Poems of Early Buddhist Nuns

Pali Text Society

Poems of Early Buddhist Nuns

(Therīgāthā)

translated by

Mrs C.A.F. Rhys Davids

(Psalms of the Sisters)
(revised version)

and

K.R. Norman

(Elders' Verses II)
(revised version)

Published by
THE PALI TEXT SOCIETY
OXFORD
1997

Psalms of the Sisters first published   1909

Reprinted with Psalms of the Brethren
as Psalms of the Early Buddhists   1937

Elders' Verses II first published   1971

This joint reprint (revised)   1989

Reprinted   1997

ISBN — 0 86013 289 7

Printed and bound in Great Britain by
Antony Rowe Ltd, Chippenham, Wiltshire.

LIST OF CONTENTS

INTRODUCTION

The poems translated in this book provide the earliest extant evidence of women's experience in any of the world's religious traditions. In view of the considerable interest now being shown in this area, in Religious Studies, Women's Studies, and elsewhere, the Council of the Pali Text Society hopes that it will be useful to provide a shortened paperback version of them; this may be acquired and used by students and the interested general reader more easily than are the hardback volumes in which the translations are currently to be found. This short introduction will describe the text, the translations, and the manner in which the new version has been produced; and will offer some bibliographical suggestions for further study.

The *Therīgāthā*, literally Poems or Verses of Elder Nuns, along with the *Theragāthā*, Poems of Elder Monks,[1] is included in the *Khuddaka Nikāya*, the fifth part of the second "basket" of Canonical scriptures, the *Sutta-piṭaka*. They are said to have been recited at the First Council, held very soon after the Buddha's death, usually given as 486 or 483 B.C. The dates of the Buddha are still in dispute, but all scholars and Buddhists agree that they fall somewhere between the first half of the sixth and the second quarter of the fourth centuries B.C. For this reason, and others, the dating of all ancient

---

[1] In the later tradition of Buddhist monasticism, it is only ten years after their higher ordination that a Buddhist monk or nun, *bhikkhu* or *bhikkhunī,* acquires the right to be called an Elder, *thera* or *therī.* As will be seen, some poems in this collection state that their authors had been nuns for very much shorter periods of time.

Buddhist texts is difficult: but with a very few exceptions, there seems no reason to doubt that the verses ascribed to these Elders do preserve traditions stemming from monks and nuns of the Buddha's own time or shortly thereafter. Apart from a German rendering by K.E. Neumann published in 1899, the two versions re-published here are the only two full translations of this text into a modern western language. Mrs. Rhys Davids' version was first issued in 1909 as *Psalms of the Sisters*, and was later reprinted together with her translation of *Theragāthā, Psalms of the Brethren*, the two together being called *Psalms of the Early Buddhists*. K.R. Norman's version was published in 1971 as *Elders' Verses* II, his translation of the *Theragāthā* having appeared as *Elders' Verses* I in 1969. (The two versions of the *Therīgāthā* are referred to hereafter as RhD and KRN respectively.)

RhD includes extracts (printed in smaller type than the verses) from the commentary written by Dhammapāla, who is thought to have lived in the sixth century A.D. in South India. He states that he was following the style of older commentaries, and that (like his slightly earlier predecessor the great Buddhaghosa) his explanations are those of the tradition preserved by the Mahāvihāra monastic fraternity in Ceylon. In this tradition, commentaries are said to have been brought from India to Ceylon by Emperor Aśoka's mission in the third century B.C., along with the Pali Canon; and, like the canonical texts, to have been preserved orally until the second half of the first century B.C., when the texts and commentaries were both written down for the first time. So although the commentary as we now have it dates from almost a millenium after the time of the Buddha, and although we do not know exactly which earlier commentaries Dhammapāla was using, there seems again no reason to doubt that he has preserved material from much earlier times; certainly on many occasions the commentarial stories provide a very useful context in which to understand the verses. RhD's style perhaps requires a little comment. She aimed at a poetic rendering; and in all her translations adopted what may now seem a rather enthusiastic, even florid style. On a number of occasions she incorporated into her translation of the verses explanatory elements taken from the commentary. In common with many early translators of Buddhist texts, she often chose to use a Biblical style: thus she writes, for example, of the Buddha's "Gospel", and often uses the archaic second person singulars "thou", "thee", and "thine". In particular, it should be noted that one of her most characteristic terms, "the Norm" is a translation of the Buddhist word *dhamma* (Sanskrit *dharma*). A few moments' reflection should be enough to remind the modern reader of the very great differences between the styles and usages of our own time and those which were appropriate in the cultural circumstances of a woman scholar in England in 1909, five years before the First World War and nineteen years before all women over 21 were granted the right to vote (it was given to women over 30 in 1918). Allowances for these differences and appropriate adaptations of her work can then easily be made. For this edition we have made minimal alterations to her version: we have corrected obvious typographical errors, made changes according to the corrigenda and errata from later editions of the work published by Mrs. Rhys Davids, and have made a few other minor changes to her punctuation and wording. At the end of her version of the *Therīgāthā* can be found a translation of verses attributed to nuns in the *Bhikkhunī-saṃyutta* of the *Saṃ-yutta-Nikāya*. This was published as an appendix to the original edition of *Psalms of the Sisters,* and then again with some emendations and additional notes in her translation of the first eleven sections of the *Saṃyutta*, published as *Kindred Sayings* vol. I. We have retained the former version.

The style of KRN is radically different. In the Introductions to *Elders' Verses* I (p. xxxii) and II (pp. xxxviii-xxxix) he explained that his intention was to provide a prose translation to be used alongside the original Pali text. Given that for this purpose the aim was "to provide a literal, almost word-for-word, translation", naturally the English version alone may seem to be characterised by "a starkness and austerity of words". It is hoped that the combination of the two versions in this book will enable the reader without knowledge of Pali to get as close to the meaning of the text as is possible through translations (see below). For this edition, some minor changes have been made by Mr. Norman; the word *āsava*, which RhD renders "(deadly) drugs" on its first occurrence at v. 47, has been left untranslated, on the grounds that any English equivalent could only be misleading (see the discussion at *Elders' Verses* I pp. 133-34).

The two versions are often different, sometimes incompatible. These differences are on occasion the result of differences in interpretation, but more often of the many advances made in Buddhist scholarship in the intervening period, in lexicography, metrical analysis and other fields. Most importantly, the editions of the text of both the *Therīgāthā* and Dhammapāla's commentary from which Mrs.

Rhys Davids worked were defective in some places. A second edition of the text of the *Thera-* and *Therīgāthā* was published in 1966, with an appendix by Mr. Norman containing alternative readings for *Theragāthā*; a similar list of alternative readings for *Therīgāthā* can be found on pp.197-99 of *Elders' Verses* II. The commentary was originally published in 1893 in an edition by E. Müller, but it is so unreliable that, unlike almost all of its other publications, the PTS has decided not to keep it in print. It is hoped that a new edition and translation will be produced in the near future.

We suggest that the book may best be used in the following way. We have printed RhD first, since the commentarial stories set a narrative context. The two translations of the verses may then be directly compared; KRN, being the more literal, provides balance and control for the poetic and imaginative empathy attempted in RhD. The translations can stand on their own: but those who wish to study them in more depth can turn to the earlier published versions, since their Introductions, footnotes and endnotes provide, obviously, a great deal of useful explanatory detail. (This would be advisable also for teachers reading the book with a class of students.) A small example: some verses contain puns on the nun's name, which RhD has on occasion tried to retain. In verse 2, the name Muttā means "Freed" and is etymologically connected with well-known and widely used Indian and Buddhist words for "freedom" or "liberation" (*mukti, mokṣa*, etc.); RhD thus translates it as "Liberta"; in verse 3, however, there is a similar pun on the name Puṇṇā, meaning "full", but since she found no obvious English counterpart it is simply transliterated.

It is an old cliché that "poetry is what gets lost in translation": in the end, for any students or others wishing to study these poems in real depth, it will be necessary to learn Pali. For this purpose, A.K. Warder's *Introduction to Pali* is now available in paperback, with an added key to the earlier untranslated exercises, making it possible to use the book as a "Teach Yourself" primer. The Society's Pali-English Dictionary, edited by T.W. Rhys Davids and W. Stede, is still in print and being sold at a reduced price. It is hoped that in about five years from now, a revised and enlarged edition of the Dictionary will also be available. Many of the linguistic puzzles and problems in the *Therīgāthā* can only be discussed in relation to the metre in which the verses are written. Warder's *Pali Metre* will help those who wish to investigate this aspect. (KRN's Introduction and notes also contain a great deal of metrical analysis and information.)

The *Therīgāthā* and Dhammapāla's commentary are discussed in histories of Indian and Buddhist literature: see, for example, K.R. Norman's *Pāli Literature*, W. Geiger's *Pāli Language and Literature*, M. Winternitz's *History of Indian Literature*, and G.P. Malalasekera's *Pāli Literature of Ceylon*. Many of the nuns whose verses and stories are given here are also mentioned in other texts: Malalasekera's *Dictionary of Pāli Proper Names* provides summary biographies; M.H. Bode translated some stories from the commentary to the *Aṅguttara Nikāya*, while E.W. Burlinghame's translation of the commentary to the *Dhammapada* also contains many versions of their stories as well as much other narrative material of the same genre. There have been very few studies of the

Therīgāthā from a literary critical point of view; but mention may be made of the article by S. Lienhard, which discusses similarities between these poems and other, non-religious poetry in Sanskrit and Prakrit, and includes a consideration of Ambapāli's verses (vv. 252-70). Recently K. Lang has made a comparative study of the nuns' and monks' poems, and argues that there are differences between them, particularly in relation to their attitudes to the body.

WORKS CITED IN THE INTRODUCTION

Unless otherwise specified, all works are published by the PTS and are still in print. The dates given are the first date of publication by the PTS.

Burlinghame, E.W., *Buddhist Legends*, 1969

Bode, M.H., "Women Leaders of the Buddhist Revolution", *Journal of the Royal Asiatic Society*, 1893, pp. 517-66, 763-98

Geiger, W., *Pāli Literature and Language* (English translation incorporating new material), Calcutta 1943

Lang, K.C., "Lord Death's Snare: gender-related imagery in the Theragāthā and Therīgāthā", *Journal of Feminist Studies in Religion,* 1986, vol. II no. 2, pp. 63-79

Lienhard, S., "Sur la structure poétique des Theratherīgāthā", *Journal Asiatique*, 1975, Tome CCLXIII, Fasc. 3-4, pp. 375-96

Malalasekera, G.P., *Pāli Literature of Ceylon*, Colombo 1928
Dictionary of Pāli Proper Names, 2 vols., 1938

Müller, E., *Therīgāthā Commentary*, 1893 (out of print)

Norman, K.R., *Elders' Verses* I, 1969
      Elders' Verses II, 1971
      Pāli Literature, Wiesbaden 1983
Rhys Davids, C.A.F., *Kindred Sayings*, vol. I, 1917
      Psalms of the Early Buddhists, 1937
Rhys Davids, T.W. and Stede, W., *Pali-English Dictionary*,
      1921-25
Thera-Therī-gāthā, edited by H. Oldenberg and R. Pischel, 2nd.
      ed. with appendices by K.R. Norman and L. Alsdorf,
      1966
Warder, A.K., *Introduction to Pali*, 2nd. ed., 1974
      Pali Metre, 1967
Winternitz, M., *History of Indian Literature*, vol. II, (English
      translation with author's additions), Calcutta 1933

Steven Collins
February 1989

THE COMMENTATOR'S INTRODUCTION

Honour to that Exalted One, Arahant, Very Buddha !

Now is the occasion come for commenting on the meaning of the psalms of the Sisters. The exposition of their several poems will be made easier and more intelligible, if I first relate the circumstances under which the Bhikkhunīs in the beginning came to leave the world and obtain admission into the Order. Of this, therefore, I will give an account in outline.

When the Lord of the world had combined the Eight Factors — humanity and the rest of Buddhahood — when, having made his great resolve at the feet of the Buddha Dīpaṅkara, and mastering equally all the Thirty Perfections, according to the prophecy of the Four-and-Twenty Buddhas in succession concerning him, he had reached the climax in his progress towards wisdom, knowledge of the world and Buddhahood, then he took rebirth in the Realms of Bliss (*Tusita*). And there, when he had lived the span of life among the ten thousand gods of the Cosmic Circles, he thereupon assented to the request of those gods to be reborn as a man that he might become a Buddha, according to their words:

'The time is now at hand when Thou,
Great Hero, shouldst as man be born,
Bearing both gods and me across,
Do Thou reveal th' Ambrosial Way!'

So He made the Five Great Considerations, and then, in the house of King Suddhodana, of the princely clan of the Sākiyas, did he, mindful and self-possessed, enter a mother's womb; then, mindful and self-possessed, did he there ten months abide; then, mindful and self-possessed, did he thence emerge and come to birth in the Lumbinī Grove.

Reared by divers nurses, surrounded ever in luxury by a great retinue, he grew up in due course, dwelling in one of three mansions, amid divers bands of nautch-women, and enjoying

honours like a god. Then, anguish being stirred in him at sight of
an aged man, a diseased man, and a dead man, he, from the
maturity of his insight, saw the danger in the life of the senses and
the profit in renouncing it. Mounting his horse Kanthaka, and
with Channa as his companion, at midnight, through the gate set
open by spirits, he went forth on the Great Renunciation. During
the remainder of that night he traversed three kingdoms, and
coming to the bank of the river Anomā, and taking the outward
marks of an Arahant, brought to him by the Brahma-god
Ghaṭīkāra, he left the world. Thereupon, as though he were
already an Elder with the eight requisites, comely in appearance
and of graceful deportment, he came in due course to Rājagaha,
and there going round for alms, he ate his meal in the cave of
Mount Paṇḍava. There the King of Magadha offered him his
kingdom. But he, refusing it, went to Bhaggava's hermitage and
learnt his system; thence to Āḷāra and Uddaka and learnt their
systems. Finding all that inadequate, he proceeded to Uruvelā, and
there for six years practised austerites. Then, discerning that this
brought no penetration of the Ariyan Norm, he said, 'This is not
the Path to Enlightenment,' and, taking solid food, he in a few
days recovered strength. So, on full-moon day in the month of
May, he ate the choice food given by Sujātā, and, casting the
golden dish upstream into the river, he, full of his resolve, 'To-
day will I become a Buddha !', ascended at eventide the Bo-tree
seat — his praises sung by Kāla, king of the Nāgas — and there,
in a quakeless spot facing the eastern world, seated him cross-
legged and indomitable. There, fixing his will in four respects, he
vanquished the power of Māra ere the sun went down. In the first
watch of the night he recalled his former lives; in the middle watch
he purified the eye celestial; in the last watch he sounded the depth
of the knowledge of the Causal Law. And, grasping in direct and
reverse order the formula of causal relation, he developed insight,
and reached that perfect enlightenment reached by all Buddhas but
shared by no one else. There then abiding seven days in the
Fruition which has Nibbāna as its object, and, in the same
manner, abiding yet other seven days on the Bo-tree seat, he
partook of sweet food beneath the Rājāyatana tree. Then, again,

seated beneath the Goatherds' Banyan, he reflected on the depth of the essence of the Norm. And his mind was disinclined for effort till he was entreated by Great Brahmā; but then he gazed upon the world with the Buddha-Eye, and, seeing all the diverse range of faculties in all beings, he promised Great Brahmā that he would teach the Norm. Meditating, 'Where, now, shall I first teach the Norm ?' he discerned that Ālāra and Uddaka had passed away; but then he thought, 'Very helpful to me were the Five who were attending on me when I broke off from my ascetic struggles.What if I were first to preach to them ?' So, in the full moon of July, he went from the Great Bo-tree toward Benares. And when he had travelled eighteen leagues, he met halfway the recluse Upaka and conversed with him; and so on to Isipatana where he convinced the Five by means of the Discourse called Turning the Wheel of the Norm, beginning:

'There are two ends, O bhikkhus, which the man who has given up the world ought not to follow ... '

thus giving them, beginning with Aññakondañña, together with eighteen myriads of Brahma-gods, a draught of Truth-ambrosia. Then on the first day of the next fortnight he established also Elder Bhaddaji in the path of the Stream-winners; on the second day, Elder Vappa; on the third day, Elder Mahānāma; on the fourth, Elder Assaji; and on the fifth day, by preaching the sermon of No Marks of the Self, he established them all in Arahantship. Thereafter he brought over many folk into the Ariyan fold — to wit, the fifty-five youths led by Yasa, the thirty Bhaddavaggiyans in the Cotton-tree Grove, and the thousand former ascetics on the ridge of Gayā-Head. And when he had established eleven myriads, with Bimbisāra at their head, in the fruit of Entering the Stream (conversion), and one myriad in the Three Refuges, he accepted the gift of the Bamboo Grove, and there abode. Now when Sāriputta and Moggallāna, brought into the First Path through Assaji, had taken leave of Sañjaya (their teacher), had joined the Buddha with their respective followings, and had realized the topmost Fruition, he set them, who had attained the perfection of discipleship, over all his disciples. Then, going at the entreaty of Elder Kāḷudāyi to Kapilavatthu, he subdued the proud stubbornness of his kinsmen by the Twin Miracle, and establishing his father in the Path of No-Return, and Great Pajāpatī in the Fruition of Entering the Stream, and causing the princes Nanda, and Rāhula to renounce the world, he went back to Rājagaha.

Now it came thereafter to pass, while the Master was staying at the Hall of the Gabled House near Vesālī, that King Suddhodana attained Arahantship while under the white canopy, and then passed away. Then in Great Pajāpatī arose the thought of renouncing the world. Then there came to her the wives of those five hundred young nobles who had renounced the world on hearing, on the bank of the Rohiṇī river, the 'Discourse concerning Strife and Dissension,' and they told her, saying: 'We will all renounce the world to follow the Master.' And they wished that she should lead them to him. Now Great Pajāpatī had once already asked the Master for admission to his Order, and had not won his consent; wherefore she now bade her hairdresser cut off her hair, and donning the yellow robes, she took all those Sākiya ladies with her to Vesālī, and there entreating Him of the Tenfold Power through Elder Ānanda, she gained his permission to leave the world and enter the Order by accepting the Eight Rules. And the others, also, were all ordained at the same time.

This, in brief, is the story. What is here said has been handed down at greater length here and there in the Pali Canon.

Thus ordained, Great Pajāpatī came before the Master, and, saluting him, stood on one side. Then he taught her the Norm. She, taking up under him the system of exercise, attained to Arahantship. The other five hundred Bhikkhunīs attained it at the end of Nandaka's sermon. Now the Order of Bhikkhunīs being thus well established, and multiplying in divers villages, towns, country districts, and royal residences, dames, daughters-in-law and maidens of the clans, hearing of the great enlightenment of the Buddha, of the very truth of the Norm, of the excellent practices of the Order, were mightily pleased with the system, and, dreading the round of rebirth, they sought permission of husband, parents, and kin, and taking the system to their bosom, renounced the world. So renouncing and living virtuously, they received instruction from the Master and the Elders, and with toil and effort soon realized Arahantship. And the psalms which they uttered from time to time, in bursts of enthusiasm and otherwise, were afterwards by the Recensionists included in the Rehearsal, and arranged together in eleven cantos. They are called the Verses of the Elder Women (Therīgāthā), and they are divided into cantos of single verses, two verses, and so on, as follows:

CANTO I

PSALMS OF SINGLE VERSES

I

Verse uttered by a certain Sister, a Bhikkhunī of Name Unknown.

Sleep softly, little Sturdy, take thy rest
At ease, wrapt in the robe thyself hast made.
Stilled are the passions that would rage within,
Withered as potherbs in the oven dried. (1)

How was she reborn ?

Long ago, a certain daughter of one of the clans became a fervent believer in the teaching of the Buddha Koṇāgamana and entertained him hospitably. She had an arbour made with boughs, a draped ceiling, and a sanded floor, and did him honour with flowers and perfumes. And all her life doing meritorious acts, she was reborn among the gods, and then again among men when Kassapa was Buddha, under whom she renounced the world. Reborn again in heaven till this Buddha-dispensation, she was finally born in a great nobleman's family at Vesālī. From the study build of her body they called her Sturdykin. She became the devoted wife of a young noble. When the Master came to Vesālī, she was convinced by his teaching, and became a lay-disciple. Anon, hearing the Great Pajāpatī the Elder preaching the Doctrine, the wish arose in her to leave the world, and she told this to her husband. He would not consent; so she went on performing her duties, reflecting on the sweetness of the doctrine, and living devoted to insight. Then one day in the kitchen, while the curry was cooking, a mighty flame of fire shot up, and burnt all the food with much crackling. She, watching it, made it a basis for rapt meditation on the utter impermanence of all things.

Thereby she was established in the Fruition of the Path of No-Return. Thenceforth she wore no more jewels and ornaments. When her husband asked her the reason, she told him how incapable she felt of living a domestic life. So he brought her, as Visākha brought Dhammadinnā, with a large following, to Great Pajāpatī the Gotamid, and said: 'Let the reverend Sisters give her ordination', And Pajāpatī did so, and showed her the Master; and the Master, emphasizing, as was his custom, the visible basis whereby she had attained, spoke the verse above.

Now, when she had attained Arahantship, the Sister repeated that verse in her exultation, wherefore this verse became her verse.

II

Verse wherewith the Exalted One frequently exhorted Muttā while a Student.

Get free, Liberta, free e'en as the Moon
From out the Dragon's jaws sails clear on high.
Wipe off the debts that hinder thee, and so,
With heart at liberty, break thou thy fast. (2)

This is the verse of a student named Muttā. She, too, being one who had made a resolve under former Buddhas, went on heaping up good of age-enduring efficacy in this and that state of becoming. Finally she was reborn in this Buddha-dispensation as the child of an eminent brahmin at Sāvatthī, and named Muttā. And in her twentieth year, her destiny being fully ripe, she renounced the world under the Great Pajāpatī the Gotamid, and studied the exercises for ecstatic insight. Returning one day from her round for alms, she discharged her duties toward her seniors, and then going apart to rest, and seated out of sight, she began to concentrate herself. Then the Master, sitting in the 'Fragrant Chamber' of the Vihāra, sent forth glory, and revealing himself as if seated before her, uttered the verse above. And she, steadfast in that exhortation, not long after attained Arahantship, and so attaining, exulted in the words of that verse. Completing her studies and promoted to full rank, she yet again uttered it, when about to pass away.

III

Puṇṇā.

The following verse is that of a student named Puṇṇā. She, heaping up good of age-enduring efficacy under former Buddhas in this and that state of becoming, was born — when the world was empty of a Saviour Buddha — as a fairy, by the River Candabhāgā. One day she worshipped a certain Silent Buddha with a wreath of reeds. Thereby gaining heaven, she was, in this Buddha-dispensation, reborn as the child of a leading burgess of Sāvatthī and named Puṇṇā. When she had so dwelt for twenty years, her destiny then being fully ripe, she heard the Great Pajāpatī teach the doctrine, and renounced the world. Becoming a student, she began to practise insight. And the Master from the 'Fragrant Chamber' shed a glory, and spake this verse:

Fill up, Puṇṇā, the orb of holy life,
E'en as on fifteenth day the full-orb'd moon.
Fill full the perfect knowledge of the Path,
And scatter all the gloom of ignorance. (3)

Hearing this, her insight grew, and she attained Arahantship. This verse is the expression of her exultation and the affirmation of her (attainment of) wisdom.

IV

Tissā.

The following verse is that of Tissā, a student. Heaping up merit under former Buddhas, Tissā was, in this Buddha-dispensation, reborn at Kapilavatthu in the noble clan of the Sākiyas. Made a lady of the Bodhisatta's court, she renounced the world with Great Pajāpatī the Gotamid, and practised herself in insight. To her the Master appeared as to the foregoing Sisters, and said:

O Tissā ! train thyself in the trainings three.
See that the great conjuncture now at hand
Pass thee not by ! Unloose all other yokes,
And fare thou forth purged of the deadly Drugs. (4)

And she, when she heard the verse, increased in insight, and attained Arahantship. Thereafter she was wont to repeat the lines.

V-X

Another Sister Tissā.

Tissā ! lay well upon thy heart the yoke
Of noblest culture. See the moment come !
Let it not pass thee by ! for many they
Who mourn in misery that moment past. (5)

Dhīrā.

Come, O Dhīrā, reach up and touch the goal
Where all distractions cease, where sense is stilled.

Where dwelleth bliss; win thou Nibbāna, win
That sure Salvation which hath no beyond. (6)

Another Sister Dhīrā.

Dhīrā, brave Sister ! who hath valiantly
Thy faculties in noblest culture trained,
Bear to this end thy last incarnate frame,
For thou hast conquered Māra and his host. (7)

Mittā.

Mittā, thou Sister friend ! who camest forth
Convinced in heart, love thou in thought and deed
Friends worthy of thy love. So train thyself
In ways of good to win the safe, sure Peace. (8)

Bhadrā.

Bhadrā, who camest forth convinced in heart,
To sure felicity, O fortunate !
That heart devote. Develop all that's good,
Faring to uttermost Security. (9)

Upasamā.

Upasamā ! cross thou serene and calm
The raging difficult Flood where death doth reign.
Bear to this end thy last incarnate frame,
For thou hast vanquished Māra and his host. (10)

Of all of these six Sisters the story is similar to that of
Tissā (IV), with this exception: Dhīrā, called 'another Sister
Dhīrā,' had no glory-verse pronounced to her, but was troubled in
heart at the Master's teaching. Leaning on his words, she strove
for insight, and when she had reached Arahantship, she declaimed
her verse in exultation. All the others did the same.

XI

Muttā.

Muttā, heaping up good under former Buddhas, was, in this
Buddha-dispensation, born in the land of Kosala as the daughter of
a poor brahmin named Oghātaka. Come to proper age, she was
given to a hunchbacked brahmin; but she told him she could not
continue in the life of the house, and induced him to consent to her
leaving the world. Exercising herself in insight, her thoughts still
ran on external objects of interest. So she practised self-control,
and, repeating her verse, strove after insight till she won
Arahantship; then exulting, she repeated:

O free, indeed ! O gloriously free
Am I in freedom from three crooked things:
From quern, from mortar, from my crookback'd lord.
Ay, but I'm free from rebirth and from death,
And all that dragged me back is hurled away. (11)

XII

Dhammadinnā.

Now, she, in the time when Padumuttara was Buddha, lived at Haṃsavatī in a state of servitude; and because she ministered and did honour to one of the chief apostles when he rose from his cataleptic trance, she was reborn in heaven and so on, among gods and men, till Phussa was Buddha. Then she worked merit by doubling the gift prescribed by her husband to the Master's half-brothers while they were staying in a servant's house. And when Kassapa was Buddha, she came to birth in the house of Kiki, King of Kāsī as one of the Seven Sisters, his daughters, and for 20,000 years lived a holy life. ... Finally, in this Buddha-dispensation, she was reborn of a clansman's family at Rājagaha, and became the wife of Visākha, a leading citizen. Now one day her husband went to hear the Master teaching, and became One-who-returns-no-more. When he came home, Dhammadinnā met him as he went up the stairs; but he leant not on her outstretched hand, nor spoke to her at supper. And she asked: 'Dear sir, why did you not take my hand ? Why do you not talk to me ? Have I done anything amiss ?' ''Tis for no fault in you, Dhammadinnā; but from henceforth I am not fit to touch a woman or take pleasure in food, for of such is the doctrine now borne in upon me. Do you according as you wish, either continuing to dwell here, or taking as much wealth as you need and going back to your family.' 'Nay, dear sir, I will make no such going back. Suffer me to leave the world.' 'It is well, Dhammadinnā', replied Visākha, and sent her to the Bhikkhunīs in a golden palanquin. Admitted to the Order, she shortly after asked permission of her teachers to go into retreat, saying: 'Mothers, my heart hath no delight in a place of crowds; I would go into a village abode.' The Bhikkhunīs brought her thither, and while there, because in her past lives she had subjugated the complexities of thought, word, and deed, she soon attained Arahantship, together with thorough mastery of the form and meaning of the Dhamma. Thereupon she thought: 'Now have

I reached the summit. What shall I do here any longer ? I will even go to Rājagaha and worship the Master, and many of my kinsfolk will, through me, acquire merit.' So she returned with her Bhikkhunīs. Then Visākha hearing of her return, curious to know why she came, interviewed her with questions on the Khandhas and the like. And Dhammadinnā answered every question as one might cut a lotus-stalk with a knife, and finally referred him to the Master. The Master praised her great wisdom, as it is told in the Lesser Vedalla (Miscellany) Sutta, and ranked her foremost among the Sisters who could preach. But it was while she was dwelling in the country, and, while yet in the lowest path, was acquiring insight to reach the highest, that she uttered her verse:

In whom desire to reach the final rest
Is born suffusing all the mind of her,
Whose heart by lure of sense-desire no more
Is held, Bound Upstream: so shall she be called. (12)

XIII

Visākhā.

Her story is similar to that of the Sister Dhīrā. After winning Arahantship she pondered on the bliss of emancipation, and thus announced her (attainment of) wisdom:

The Buddha's will be done ! See that ye do
His will. An ye have done it, never more
Need ye repent the deed. Wash, then, in haste
Your feet and sit ye down aloof, alone. (13)

Thus she admonished others to follow her example.

XIV

Sumanā.

Her story is similar to that of Sister Tissā. Sending forth glory, the Master revealed himself as if seated in front of her, and spake:

Hast thou not seen sorrow and ill in all
The springs of life ? Come thou not back to birth !
Cast out the passionate desire again to Be.
So shalt thou go thy ways calm and serene. (14)

XV

Uttarā.

Her story is also similar to that of Sister Tissā. And it was the 'Glory-verse' through which she won Arahantship that she declaimed in exultation:

Well have I disciplined myself in act,
In speech and eke in thought, rapt and intent.
Craving with root of craving is o'ercome;
Cool am I now; I know Nibbāna's peace. (15)

XVI

Sumanā.
(Who left the world when old)

She too, having made her resolve under former Buddhas, and heaping up good in this life and in that, was, in this Buddha-dispensation, born at Sāvatthī as the sister of the King of Kosala.

Hearing the Master preach the doctrine to the King Pasenadi in the discourse beginning, 'There are four young creatures, sire, who may not be disregarded', she believed, and was established in the Refuges and the Precepts. Fain to leave the world, she put off doing so that she might take care of her grandmother as long as she lived. After the grandmother's death, Sumanā went, accompanied by the King, to the Vihāra, taking much treasure in carpets and shawls, and presenting them to the Order. And hearing the Master teach, she attained the fruit of the Path of No-return, and asked for ordination. And the Master, discerning the maturity of her knowledge, spake thus:

Happily rest, thou venerable dame!
Rest thee, wrapt in the robe thyself hast made.
Stilled are the passions that have raged within.
Cool art thou now, knowing Nibbāna's peace. (16)

And when he had finished, she won Arahantship, together with thorough knowledge of the Norm in form and in meaning. In her exultation she uttered that same verse, so that it became the announcement of her (attainment of) wisdom. Straightway she left the world for the Order.

XVII

Dhammā.

She, too, having made her resolve under former Buddhas, and heaping up merit in this and that state of becoming, was, in this Buddha-dispensation, born in a respectable family at Sāvatthī. Given in marriage to a suitable husband, she became converted, and desired to leave the world, but her husband would not consent. So she waited till after his death, and then entered the Order. One day, returning to the Vihāra from seeking alms, she lost her balance and fell. Making just that her base of insight, she won

Arahantship with thorough knowledge of the Norm in form and in meaning. And, triumphing, she uttered this verse:

Far had I wandered for my daily food;
Weary with shaking limbs I reached my rest,
Leaning upon my staff, when even there
I fell to earth. Lo ! all the misery
Besetting this poor mortal frame lay bare
To inward vision. Prone the body lay;
The heart of me rose up in liberty. (17)

XVIII

Saṅghā.

Her story is like that of Sister Dhīrā, but her verse is as follows:

Home have I left, for I have left my world !
Child have I left, and all my cherish'd herds !
Lust have I left, and Ill-will, too, is gone,
And Ignorance have I put far from me;
Craving and root of Craving overpowered,
Cool am I now, knowing Nibbāna's peace. (18)

CANTO II

PSALMS OF TWO VERSES

XIX

Abhirūpa-Nandā.

Born in the time of the Buddha Vipassi, in his native town of Bandhumatī, as the daughter of a wealthy burgess, she became a pious lay-adherent, and at the Master's death she made an offering to the shrine of his ashes of a golden umbrella surrounded with jewels. Reborn for this in various heavens, she was, in this Buddha-dispensation, reborn at Kapilavatthu as the daughter of a chief wife of Khemaka, the Sākiyan, and named Nandā. But because of her excessive beauty, charm, and loveliness, she was known as Nandā the Fair.

Now, on the day when she was to choose among her suitors, Carabhūta, her young Sākiyan kinsman, died. Then her parents made her leave the world against her will. But she, even after she had entered the Order, was infatuated with her own beauty, and, fearing the Master's rebuke, avoided his presence. Now the Exalted One knew that she was ripe for knowledge, and directed the Great Pajāpatī to let all the Bhikkhunīs come to him for instruction. Nandā sent another in her place. And the Exalted One said, 'Let no one come by proxy.' So she was compelled to come. And the Exalted One, by his mystic power, conjured up a beautiful woman, and showed her becoming aged and fading, causing anguish to arise in Nandā. And he addressed her in these words:

Behold, Nandā, the foul compound, diseased,
Impure ! Compel thy heart to contemplate
What is not fair to view. So steel thyself
And concentrate the well-composed mind. (19)

That ponder where no Threefold Sign is seen.
Cast out the baneful bias of conceit.
Hath the mind mastered vain imaginings,
Then mayst thou go thy ways, calm and serene. (20)

And when he had finished speaking, she attained
Arahantship. Repeating to herself the verses, she made them the
announcement of her (attainment of) wisdom.

XX

Jentī (or Jentā).

The story of her past and present is like that of Nandā the
Fair; but it was at Vesālī in the princely family of the Licchavis,
that she was reborn. There is this further difference: she attained
Arahantship after hearing the Master preach the Dhamma, and it
was when reflecting on the change that had come over her that
she, in joy, uttered these verses:

The Seven Factors of the awakened mind,
Seven ways whereby we may Nibbāna win,
All, all have I developed and made ripe,
Even according to the Buddha's word. (21)
For I therein have seen as with mine eyes
The Bless'd, the Exalted One. Last of all lives
Is this that makes up Me. The round of births
Is vanquished — Ne'er shall I be again ! (22)

XXI

Sumaṅgala's Mother.

She, too, having made her resolve under former Buddhas, and heaping up good in this rebirth and that, was born under this Buddha-dispensation in a poor family at Sāvatthī, and was married to a rush-plaiter. Her first-born was a son, come for the last time to birth, who grew up to become the Elder Sumaṅgala and an Arahant. And her name not becoming known, she was called in the Pali text a certain unknown Therī and is known as Sumaṅgala's mother. She became a Bhikkhunī, and one day, while reflecting on all she had suffered as a lay-woman, she was much affected, and, her insight quickening, she attained Arahantship, with thorough knowledge of the form and meaning of the Dhamma. Thereupon she exclaimed:

O woman well set free ! how free am I,
How throughly free from kitchen drudgery !
Me stained and squalid 'mong my cooking-pots
My brutal husband ranked as even less
Than the sunshades he sitting weaves alway. (23)

Purged now of all my former lust and hate,
I dwell, musing at ease beneath the shade
Of spreading boughs — O, but 'tis well with me ! (24)

XII

Aḍḍhakāsī.

Born of a respectable family, in the time of Kassapa Buddha, she won understanding, and became a Bhikkhunī, established in the precepts. But she reviled an Arahant Elder Sister by calling her a prostitute, and for this she went to purgatory. In this Buddha-dispensation she was reborn in the kingdom of Kāsī as the child of a distinguished and prosperous citizen. But because of the persistent effect of her former evil speech, she became herself a prostitute. How she left the world and was ordained by special messenger is related in the Culla Vagga. For she wished to go to Sāvatthī to be ordained by the Exalted One. But the libertines of Benares barred the ways, so she sent and asked the Exalted One's advice, and he permitted her to be ordained by a messenger. Then she, working at insight, not long after obtained Arahantship, with thorough knowedge of the Dhamma in form and meaning. Thereupon she exclaimed:

No less my fee was than the Kāsī realm
Paid in revenue — this was based on that,
Value for value — so the sheriff fixed. (25)

But irksome now is all my loveliness;
I weary of it, disillusionized.
Ne'er would I more, again and yet again,
Run on the round of rebirth and of death !
Now real and true for me the Triple Lore.
Accomplished is the bidding of the Lord. (26)

XXIII

Cittā.

She, too, having made her resolve under former Buddhas, and heaping up good of age-enduring efficacy in this rebirth and that, was born in the 94th aeon as a fairy. She worshipped with offering of flowers a Silent (Pacceka) Buddha. And after many other births among men and gods, she was, in this Buddha-dispensation, born at Rājagaha in the family of a leading burgess. When she had come to years of discretion she heard the Master teaching at the gate of Rājagaha and, becoming a believer, she was ordained by the Great Pajāpatī the Gotamid. And at length, in her old age, when she had climbed the Vulture's Peak, and had done the exercises of a recluse, her insight expanded, and she won to Arahantship. Reflecting thereon, she gave utterance as follows:

Though I be suffering and weak, and all
My youthful spring be gone, yet have I climbed,
Leaning upon my staff, the mountain crest. (27)
Thrown from my shoulder hangs my cloak, o'er-turned
My little bowl. So 'gainst the rock I lean
And prop this self of me, and break away
The wildering gloom that long had closed me in. (28)

XXIV

Mettikā.

Heaping up merit under former Buddhas, she was born during the time of Siddhattha, the Exalted One, in a burgess's family, and worshipped at his shrine by offering there a jewelled girdle. After many births in heaven and on earth, through the merit thereof, she became, in this Buddha-dispensation, the child of an eminent brahmin at Rājagaha. In other respects her case is like the preceding one, save that it was another hill corresponding to Vulture's Peak up which she climbed.

She, too, reflecting on what she had won, said in exultation:

Though I be suffering and weak, and all
My youthful spring be gone, yet have I come,
Leaning upon my staff, and climbed aloft
The mountain peak. (29)

My cloak thrown off,
My little bowl o'erturned: so sit I here
Upon the rock. And o'er my spirit sweeps
The breath of Liberty ! I win, I win
The Triple Lore ! The Buddha's will is done ! (30)

XXV

Mittā.

Born in the time of Vipassi Buddha of a noble family, and become a
lady of his father's court, she won meritorious karma by
bestowing food and precious raiment on an Arahant Elder Sister.
Born finally, in this Buddha-dispensation, in the princely family of
the Sākiyas, at Kapilavatthu she left the world together with
Great Pajāpatī the Gotamid and, going through the requisite
training for insight, not long after won Arahantship. Reflecting
thereon, joy and gladness stirred her to say:

On full-moon day and on the fifteenth day,
And eke the eighth of either half the month,
I kept the feast; I kept the precepts eight,
The extra fasts, enamoured of the gods,
And fain to dwell in homes celestial. (31)

To-day one meal, head shaved, a yellow robe —
Enough for me. I want no heaven of gods.
Heart's pain, heart's pining, have I trained away. (32)

XXVI

Abhaya's Mother.

Heaping up merit under former Buddhas, she, in the time of
Tissa Buddha, saw him going round for alms, and with glad heart
took his bowl and placed in it a spoonful of food. Reborn for that
among gods and among men, she was born also for that, in this
Buddha-dispensation, and became the town belle of Ujjenī, by
name Padumavatī. And King Bimbisāra (of Magadha) heard of her,
and expressed to his chaplain the wish to see her. By the power of
his spells, the chaplain summoned a Yakkha who, by his might,
brought the King to Ujjenī. And when she afterwards sent word to
the King that she was with child by him, he sent back word,
saying: 'If it be a son, let me see him when he is grown.' And she
bore a son and called him Abhaya. When he was seven years old
she told him who was his father, and sent him to Bimbisāra. The
King loved the boy, and let him grow up with the boys of his
court. His conversion and ordination is told in the Psalms of the
Elders. And, later on, his mother heard her son preach the
Dhamma, and she, too, left the world and afterwards attained
Arahantship, with thorough grasp of the Dhamma in form and
meaning. She thereupon recalled and repeated the verse wherewith
her son had admonished her, and added her own thereto:

Upward from sole of foot, O mother dear,
Downward from crown of hair this body see.
Is't not impure, the evil-smelling thing ? (33)
This have I pondered, meditating still,
Till every throb of lust is rooted out.
Expunged is all the fever of desire.
Cool am I now and calm — Nibbāna's peace. (34)

XXVII

Abhayā.

She, too, having made her resolve under former Buddhas, and heaping up merit of age-enduring efficacy in this and that state of becoming, was, in the time of Sikhi Buddha, reborn in a great noble's family, and became the chief queen of his father Aruṇa. And one day she worshipped the Exalted One with offering of red lotuses given her by the King, when Sikhi Buddha, at alms-time, entered the palace. Reborn for this among gods and men, she was, in this Buddha-dispensation, born once more at Ujjenī in a respectable family, and became the playmate of Abhaya's mother. And when the latter had left the world, Abhayā for love of her, also took orders. Dwelling with her at Rājagaha, she went one day to Cool-Grove to contemplate on a basis of some foul thing. The Master, seated in his Fragrant Chamber, caused her to see before her the kind of object she had been directed to choose. Seeing the vision, dread seized her. Then the Master, sending forth glory, appeared as if seated before her, and said:

Brittle, O Abhayā, the body is,
Whereto the worldling's happiness is bound.
For me I shall lay down this mortal frame,
Mindful and self-possessed in all I do. (35)
For all my heart was in the work whereby
I struggled free from all that breedeth Ill.
Craving have I destroyed, and brought to pass
That which the Buddhas have revealed to men. (36)

And when he had finished speaking she attained Arahantship. Exulting herein, she turned the verses round into an address to herself.

XXVIII

Sāmā.

She, too, having made her resolve under former Buddhas, and heaping up good of age-enduring efficacy in this and that state of becoming, being reborn in fortunate conditions, took birth, in this Buddha-dispensation, at Kosambī, in the family of an eminent burgess. When her dear friend, the lay-disciple Sāmāvatī, died, she, in her distress, left the world. But being unable to subdue her grief for her friend, she was unable to grasp the Ariyan Way. Now, while she was seated in the sitting-room, listening to Elder Ānanda preaching, she was established in insight, and, on the seventh day after, attained Arahantship, with thorough grasp of the Dhamma in form and meaning.

And reflecting on what she had won, she expressed it in this psalm:

Four times, nay, five, I sallied from my cell,
And roamed afield to find the peace of mind
I sought in vain, and governance of thoughts
I could not bring into captivity. (37)
To me, even to me, on that eighth day
It came: all craving ousted from my heart.
'Mid many sore afflictions, I had wrought
With passionate endeavour, and had won !
Craving was dead, and the Lord's will was done. (38)

CANTO III

PSALMS OF THREE VERSES

XXIX

Another Sāmā.

She also, heaping up good like the foregoing, was born, in the time of Vipassi Buddha, as a fairy on the banks of the River Candabhāgā. Devoted to fairy pastimes, she saw one day the Master walking on the bank, that he might sow the good seed among creatures. And with great glee she worshipped, offering flowers. For this she gained rebirth among gods and men, till, in this Buddha-dispensation, she took birth in a clansman's family at Kosambī. She too became the friend of Sāmāvatī, and she too, out of grief at the death of the latter, entered the Order. She too could not gain self-mastery for twenty-five years, till in her old age she heard a timely sermon, through which her insight expanded and she won Arahantship, with thorough grasp of the Dhamma in form and meaning. Thereon reflecting, she broke forth:

Full five-and-twenty years since I came forth !
But in my troubled heart in no way yet
Could I discern the calm of victory. (39)
The peace of mind, the governance of thoughts
Long sought, I found not; and with anguish thrilled
I dwelt in memory on the Conqueror's word. (40)
To free my path from all that breedeth Ill
I strove with passionate ardour, and I won !
Craving is dead, and the Lord's will is done.
To-day is now the seventh day since first
Was withered up within that ancient Thirst. (41)

XXX

Uttamā.

She, too, heaping up good under former Buddhas, was in the
time of Vipassi Buddha, born at Bandhumatī, in the house of a
certain wealthy landowner, and became a domestic servant. Grown
up, she tended her master's household. Now, at that time, King
Bandhumā (Vipassi's father), having restored Sabbath-keeping,
gave gifts before dining and, after dining, attended a sermon; and
the people, following his pious example, and keeping Sabbath, the
slave thought: 'Why should not I, too, do as they all are doing?'
And for the thoroughness of her observance of the feasts she was
reborn among the Three-and-Thirty gods, and in other happy
realms, and finally, in this Buddha-era, in the house of the
Treasurer of Sāvatthī. Come to years of discretion, she heard
Paṭācārā preach, and entered the Order; but she was unable to
attain the climax of insight till Paṭācārā, seeing the state of her
mind, gave her admonition. Thereby established, she won
Arahantship, with thorough grasp of the Norm in form and in
meaning. And reflecting thereon, she exulted thus:

Four times, nay, five, I sallied from my cell,
And roamed afield to find the peace of mind
Long vainly sought, and governance of thoughts
I could not bring into captivity. (42)
To me she came, that noble Bhikkhunī,
Who was my foster-mother in the faith.
She taught to me the Norm, wherein I learnt
The nature of this transitory self. (43)
And well I minded all, e'en as she taught.
For seven days I sat in Jhāna-joy
And ease, cross-legged; on the eighth day at last

I stretched my limbs, and went my way serene,
For I had burst asunder the surrounding gloom. (44)

Now, this was the affirmation of her (attainment of)
wisdom.

XXXI

Another Uttamā.

She, too, having made her resolve under former Buddhas,
and heaping up good of age-enduring efficacy in this and that
rebirth, was born, in the time of Vipassi Buddha, as a domestic
servant, at Bandhumatī. One day, seeing an Arahant of the
Master's Order seeking alms, she gladly offered him three sweet
cakes. Through this reborn to happiness, she finally came to birth,
in this Buddha-era, in the family of an eminent brahmin in the
country of Kosala. Come to years of discretion, she heard the
Master preach while touring in the country, and leaving the world,
she soon won Arahantship, together with thorough grasp of the
Norm in form and in meaning. And reflecting thereon, she exulted
thus:

The Seven Factors of the Awakened mind,
Seven Ways whereby we may Nibbāna win,
All, all have I developed and made ripe,
Even according to the Buddha's word. (45)
Fulfilled is heart's desire: I win the Void,
I win the Signless ! Buddha's daughter I,
Born of his mouth, his blessed word, I stand,
Transported with Nibbāna's bliss alway. (46)
And all the sense-desires that fetter gods,
That hinder men, are wholly riven off.

Abolished is the infinite round of births.
Becoming cometh ne'er again for me. (47)

XXXII

Dantikā.

She, too, having made her resolve under former Buddhas,
and in this and that rebirth heaping up good of age-enduring
efficacy, was born, when the world was empty of a Buddha, as a
fairy by the River Candabhāgā. Sporting one day with the fairies,
and straying awhile, she saw a silent Buddha seated at the foot of a
tree, and adored him in faith with flower-offerings. For this she
was reborn among gods and men, and, finally, in this Buddha-era,
at Sāvatthī in the house of the King's chaplain-brahmin. Come to
years of discretion, she became a lay-believer in the Jeta Grove
[College], and, later, entered the Order under Great Pajāpatī the
Gotamid. And one day, while staying at Rājagaha, she ascended
the Vulture's Peak, after her meal, and while resting, she saw that
which she tells of in her verse, whereby she won Arahantship,
with thorough grasp of the Norm in form and in meaning. And
afterwards, thrilled with happiness at the thought of her
attainment, she exulted thus:

Coming from noonday-rest on Vulture's Peak,
I saw an elephant, his bathe performed,
Forth from the river issue. And a man, (48)
Taking his goad, bade the great creature stretch
His foot: 'Give me thy foot !' The elephant
Obeyed, and to his neck the driver sprang. (49)

I saw the untamed tamed, I saw him bent
To master's will; and marking inwardly,

I passed into the forest depths and there
I' faith I trained and ordered all my heart. (50)

XXXIII

Ubbirī.

She too, having made her resolve in the time of former
Buddhas, and heaping up, in this and that rebirth, Good valid for
an aeon of evolution, was born, in the time of Padumuttara
Buddha, at the town of Haṃsavatī in a clansman's house. Come to
years of discretion, she was left alone one day, her parents being
engaged with a party in the inner court of the house. And seeing
an Arahant approaching the house-door, she bade him 'Come in
hither, lord,' and did him homage, showing him to a seat; she then
took his bowl and filled it with food. The Elder thanked her, and
departed. But she, reborn therefore in the heaven of the Three-and-
Thirty gods, enjoying there a heavenly time and many a happy life
thereafter, was, in this Buddha-era, reborn at Sāvatthī in the
family of a very eminent burgess. And she was beautiful to see,
and was brought into the house of the King of Kosala himself.
After a few years a daughter was born to her, whom she named
Jīvā. The King saw the child, and was so pleased that he had
Ubbirī anointed as Queen. But anon the little girl died, and the
mother went daily mourning to the charnel-field. And one day she
went and worshipped the Master, and sat down; but soon she left,
and stood lamenting by the River Aciravatī. Then the Master,
seeing her from afar, revealed himself, and asked her: 'Why dost
thou weep ?' 'I weep because of my daughter, Exalted One.'
'Burnt in this cemetery are some 84,000 of thy daughters. For
which of them dost thou weep ?' And pointing out the place
where this one and that one had been laid, he said half the psalm:

O Ubbiri, who wailest in the wood,
Crying 'O Jīvā ! O my daughter dear !'
Come to thyself ! Lo, in this burying-ground
Are burnt full many a thousand daughters dear,
And all of them were named like unto her.
Now which of all those Jīvās dost thou mourn ? (51)

And she pondered with intelligence on the Norm thus taught
by the Master, and so stirred up insight that, by the charm of his
teaching and her own attainment of the requisite conditions, she
reached the topmost fruit, even Arahantship. And showing forth
the high distinction she had won, she spoke the second half of the
psalm:

Lo! from my heart the hidden shaft is gone !
The shaft that nestled there hath he removed.
And that consuming grief for my dead child
Which poisoned all the life of me is dead. (52)
To-day my heart is healed, my yearning stayed,
And all within is purity and peace.
Lo ! I for refuge to the Buddha go —
The only wise— the Order and the Norm. (53)

XXXIV

Sukkā.

She, too, having fared in the past as the foregoing Sisters,
was born in a clansman's house. Come to years of discretion, she
went with lay-women disciples to the Vihāra, and heard the
Master preach. Becoming a believer, she left the world and became
learned, proficient in the doctrine, and a ready speaker. Leading for
centuries a religious life, she yet died a worldling at heart, and was

reborn in the heaven of bliss. Again, when Vipassi was Buddha, and again when Vessabhu was Buddha, she kept the precepts, and was learned and proficient in doctrine. Again, when Kakusandha was Buddha, and yet again when Koṇāgamana was Buddha, she took Orders, and was pure in conduct, learned, and a preacher. At length, she was, in this Buddha-era, reborn at Rājagaha, in the family of an eminent burgess, and called Sukkā (bright, lustrous, 'Lucy'). Come to years of discretion, she found faith in the Master at her own home, and became a lay-disciple. But later, when she heard Dhammadinnā preach, she was thrilled with emotion, and renounced the world under her. And performing the exercises for insight, she not long after attained Arahantship, together with thorough grasp of the Norm in form and in meaning.

Thereupon, attended by 500 Bhikkhunīs, she became a great preacher. And one day, when they had been into Rājagaha for alms, and had returned and dined, they entered the Bhikkhunīs' settlement, and Sukkā, with a great company seated around her, taught the doctrine in such wise that she seemed to be giving them sweet mead to drink and sprinkling them with ambrosia. And they all listened to her rapt, motionless, intent. Thereupon the spirit of the tree that stood at the end of the Sisters' terrace was inspired by her teaching, and went out to Rājagaha, walking about the ways and the squares proclaiming her excellence, and saying:

What would ye men of Rājagaha have ?
What have ye done ? that mute and idle here
Ye lie about, as if bemused with wine,
Nor wait upon Sukkā, while she reveals
The precious gospel by the Buddha taught. (54)
The wise in heart, methinks, were fain to quaff
That life's elixir, once won never lost,
That welleth ever up in her sweet words,
E'en as the wayfarer welcomes the rain. (55)

And hearing what the tree-spirit said, the people were excited, and came to the Sister and listened attentively.

At a later period, when the Sister, at the end of her life, was completing her Nibbāna, and wished to show how the system she had taught led to salvation, she declared her (attainment of) wisdom thus:

O Child of light ! by light of truth set free
From cravings dire, firm, self-possessed, serene,
Bear to this end thy last incarnate frame,
For thou hast conquered Māra and his host. (56)

XXXV

Selā.

She, too, having fared in the past as the foregoing Sisters, was born in a clansman's house at Haṃsavatī, and was given in marriage by her parents to a clansman's son of equal birth. With him she lived happily till his death. Then, being herself advanced in years, and growing anxious as she sought to find Good, she went about from park to park, from vihāra to vihāra, with the intention of teaching religion (*dhamma*) to votaries of religion. Then one day she came up to the Bo-tree of the Master and sat down, thinking: 'If a Buddha, an Exalted One, be unequalled and peerless among men, may this one show me the miracle of Buddhahood.' Scarce had the thought arisen when the Tree blazed forth, the branches appeared as if made of gold, the horizon shone all around. And she, inspired at that sight, fell down and worshipped, and for seven days sat there. On the seventh day she performed a grand feast of offering and worship to the Buddha. By this meritorious karma she was reborn in this Buddha-era, in the kingdom of Āḷavī, as the King's daughter, and named Selā. But she was also known as 'The Āḷavikan.' When the Master converted her father, ordained him, and went with him to the city of Āḷavī, Selā, come to years of discretion but being yet unmarried, went with the King and heard the Master preach. She became a believer and a lay-disciple. Afterwards, growing anxious, she took Orders, worked her way to insight, and because of the promise in her and the maturity of her knowledge, she, crushing the formations of thought, word and deed, soon won Arahantship.

      Thereafter, as an Elder, she lived at Sāvatthī. And one day she went forth from Sāvatthī to take siesta in the Dark Grove, and sat down beneath a tree. Then Māra, alone and wishing to interrupt her privacy, approached in the guise of a stranger, saying:

Ne'er shalt thou find escape while in the world !
What profiteth thee then thy loneliness ?
Take the good things of life while yet thou mayst.
Repentance else too late awaiteth thee. (57)

      Then the Sister — thinking 'Verily, 'tis that foolish Māra who would deny me the Nibbāna that is revealed to me, and bids me choose the sensuous life. He knows not that I am an Arahant. Now will I tell him and confound him' — recited the following:

Like spears and javelins are the joys of sense
That pierce and rend the mortal frames of us.
These that thou callest 'the good things of life' —
Good of that ilk to me is nothing worth. (58)

On every hand the love of pleasure yields,
And the thick gloom of ignorance is rent
In twain. Know this, O Evil One, avaunt !
Here, O Destroyer, shalt thou not prevail. (59)

XXXVI

Somā.

She, too, having fared in the past as the foregoing Sisters, was, in the time of Sikhi Buddha, reborn in the family of an eminent noble, and, when grown up, was made the chief consort of the King Aruṇavā. The story of her past is similar to that of Sister Abhayā. The story of her present is that, in this Buddha-era, she was reborn as the daughter of the chaplain of King Bimbisāra at Rājagaha, and named Somā. Come to years of discretion, she came to believe in the Master in her own home, and became a lay-disciple. And later on, growing anxious, she entered the Order of Bhikkhunīs, and, working her way to insight, she not long after won Arahantship, with thorough grasp of the Norm in letter and in spirit.

Then, dwelling at Sāvatthī in the bliss of emancipation, she went forth one day to take siesta in the Dark Grove, and sat down beneath a tree. And Māra, alone, and wishing to interrupt her privacy, approached her, invisible and in the air, saying:

That vantage-ground the sages may attain is hard
To reach. With her two-finger consciousness
That is no woman competent to gain ! (60)

For women, from the age of seven or eight, boiling rice at all times, know not the moment when the rice is cooked, but must take some grains in a spoon and press them with two fingers; hence the expression 'two-finger' sense. Then the Elder rebuked Māra:

How should the woman's nature hinder us ?
Whose hearts are firmly set, who ever move
With growing knowledge onward in the Path ?
What can that signify to one in whom

Insight doth truly comprehend the Norm ? (61)

On every hand the love of pleasure yields,
And the thick gloom of ignorance is rent
In twain. Know this, O Evil One, avaunt !
Here, O Destroyer ! shalt thou not prevail. (62)

CANTO IV

PSALMS OF FOUR VERSES

XXXVII

Bhaddā of the Kapilas.

Now she was born in the time of Padumuttara Buddha, in a clansman's house at Haṃsavatī. Come to years of discretion, she heard the Master preach, and saw him assign a Bhikkhunī the first rank among those who could recall previous lives. Thereat she made her resolve, wishing that she, too, might acquire such a rank. Working merit all her life, she was reborn, when no Buddha had arisen, in a clansman's house at Benares, and in due course married.

Then one day, a quarrel arose between her and her sister-in-law. And the latter having given food to a Silent Buddha, Bhaddā thought, 'She will win glory for this', and taking the bowl from his hand, she filled it with mud instead of food. The people said, 'Foolish woman ! what has the Silent Buddha done to offend you ?' And she, ashamed of herself, took back the bowl, emptied and scrubbed it with scented powder, filled it with the four sweet foods, and sprinkled it on the top with ghee of the colour of a lotus-calyx. Handing it back, shining, to the Silent Buddha, she registered a prayer: 'May I have a shining body like this bowl !'

After many fortunate rebirths, she was reborn, in the time of Kassapa Buddha, at Benares, as the daughter of the wealthy treasurer. But by the fruition of her previous karma her body was of evil odour, and she was repulsive to others. Much troubled thereby, she had her ornaments made into an ingot of gold, and placed it in the Buddha's shrine, doing reverence with her hands full of lotuses. Thereby her body, even in that birth, became fragrant and sweet. As a beloved wife she did good all her life, was reborn in heaven to celestial joys, and at length took birth as the daughter of the King of Benares. There she lived gloriously, ministering to Silent Buddhas. When they passed away she was greatly troubled, and left the world for ascetic practices. Dwelling in groves, she practised Jhāna, and was reborn in the Brahma heavens, and thence into the family of a brahmin of the Kosiya clan at Sāgalā. Reared in great state, she was wedded to the young noble Pippali at the village of Mahātittha. When he renounced the world she handed over her great wealth to her kinsfolk that she too might go forth; and she dwelt five years in the Sophists' Grove, after which she was ordained by Great Pajāpatī the Gotamid. Establishing insight, she soon won Arahantship.

And she became an expert in knowledge of her past lives, through the surplus force of her resolve (made in past ages), and was herein ranked first by the Master when, seated in the Jeta Grove among the company of Ariyans, he classified the Bhikkhunīs. One day she broke forth in a Psalm, recounting all that she had wrought, accompanied by a eulogy of the virtues of the great Elder Kassapa, thus:

Son of thc Buddha and his heir is he,
Great Kassapa, master of self, serene !
The vision of far, bygone days is his,
Ay, heaven and hell no secrets hold for him. (63)
Death too of rebirth hath he won, and eke
A seer is he of mystic lore profound.
By these three arms of learning doth he stand
Thrice-wise, 'mong gods and men elect, sublime. (64)

She too, Bhaddā the Kapilan — thrice-wise
And victor over death and birth is she —
Bears to this end her last incarnate frame,
For she hath conquered Māra and his host. (65)

We both have seen, both he and I, the woe
And pity of the world, and have gone forth.
We both are Arahants with selves well tamed.
Cool are we both, ours is Nibbāna now ! (66)

CANTO V

PSALMS OF FIVE VERSES

XXXVIII

An Anonymous Sister.

She, too, having fared in the past as the foregoing Sisters, was, in this Buddha-era, reborn in the town of Devadaha, and became the nurse of Great Pajāpatī the Gotamid. Her name was Vaḍḍhesī, but the name of her family has not been handed down. When her mistress renounced the world she did the same. But for five-and-twenty years she was harassed by the lusts of the senses, winning no concentration of mind even for a moment, and bewailing her state with outstretched arms, till at length she heard Dhammadinnā preaching the Norm. Then, with her mind diverted from the senses, she fell to practising meditative exercises, and in no long time acquired the Six Powers of Intuition. And, reflecting on her attainment, she exulted thus:

For five-and-twenty years since I came forth.
Not for one moment could my heart attain
The blessedness of calm serenity. (67)
No peace of mind I found. My every thought
Was soaked in the fell drug of sense-desire.
With outstretched arms and shedding futile tears
I gat me, wretched woman, to my cell. (68)

Then poor I to this Bhikkhunī drew near,
Who was my foster-mother in the faith.
She taught to me the Norm, wherein I learnt
The factors, organs, bases of this self,

Impermanent compound. Hearing her words, (69)
Beside her I sat down to meditate.

And now I know the days of the long past,
And clearly shines the Eye Celestial, (70)
I know the thoughts of other minds, and hear
With sublimated sense the sound of things
Ineffable. The mystic potencies
I exercise; and all the deadly Drugs
That poisoned every thought are purged away.
A living truth for me this Sixfold Lore,
And the commandment of the Lord is done. (71)

XXXIX

Vimalā.
(*Formerly a Courtesan*)

She too, having fared in the past as the foregoing Sisters,
was born, in this Buddha-era, at Vesālī as the daughter of a certain
woman who earned her living by her beauty. Her name was
Vimalā. When she was grown up, and was imagining vicious
things, she saw one day the venerable Mahā-Moggallāna going
about Vesālī for alms, and feeling enamoured of him, she went to
his dwelling and sought to entice him. Some say she was
instigated to do so by sectarians. The Elder rebuked her unseemly
behaviour and admonished her, as may be read in the Psalms of the
Brethren. And she was filled with shame and self-reproach, and
became a believer and lay-sister. Later she entered the Order, and
wrestling and striving — for the root of attainment was in her —
not long after won Arahantship. Thereafter, reflecting on her
gain, she exulted thus:

How was I once puff'd up, incens'd with the bloom of my
beauty,
Vain of my perfect form, my fame and success 'midst the
people,
Fill'd with the pride of my youth, I scorned and despised
other women. (72)
Lo ! I made my body, bravely arrayed, deftly painted,
Speak for me to the lads, whilst I at the door of the harlot
Stood, like a crafty hunter, weaving his snares, ever
watchful. (73)
Yea, I bared without shame my body and wealth of
adorning;
Manifold wiles I wrought, mocking with insolent laughter.
(74)

To-day with shaven head, wrapt in my robe,
I go forth on my daily round for food;
And 'neath the spreading boughs of forest tree
I sit, and Second-Jhāna's rapture win,
Where reas'nings cease, and joy and ease remain. (75)
Now all the evil bonds that fetter gods
And men are wholly rent and cut away.
Purg'd are the Āsavas that drugg'd my heart,
Cool and content I know Nibbāna's Peace. (76)

XL

Sīhā.

She too, faring in the past as the foregoing Sisters, was in
this Buddha-era born at Vesālī as the daughter of General Sīha's
sister. And, being named after her maternal uncle, she was called

Sīhā. Come to years of discretion, she heard the Master one day
teaching the Norm to the General, and, becoming a believer,
gained her parents' consent to enter the Order. When she strove
for insight, she was unable to prevent her mind from running on
objects of external charm. Harassed thus for seven years, she
concluded, 'How shall I extricate myself from this evil living ? I
will die.' And, taking a noose, she hung it round the bough of a
tree, and, fastening it round her neck, with all the cumulative
effect of former efforts, she impelled her mind to insight. Then to
her, who was really come to her last birth, at that very moment,
through her knowledge attaining maturity, insight grew within,
and she won Arahantship, together with thorough grasp of the
Norm in form and in meaning. So, loosening the rope from her
neck, she turned back again. Established as an Arahant, she
exulted thus:

Distracted, harassed by desires of sense,
Unmindful of the 'what' and 'why' of things,
Stung and inflated by the memories
Of former days, o'er which I lacked control, (77)
Corrupting canker spreading o'er my heart,
I followed heedless dreams of happiness,
And got no even tenour to my mind,
All given o'er to dalliance with sense. (78)
So did I fare for seven weary years,
In lean and sallow mis'ry of unrest.
I, wretched, found no ease by day or night, (79)
So took a rope and plunged into the wood:
'Better for me a friendly gallows-tree !
I'll live again the low life of the world. (80)
Strong was the noose I made; and on a bough
I bound the rope and flung it round my neck,
When see ! ... my heart was set at liberty ! (81)

XLI

Sundarī-Nandā.

She, verily, was born, in the time of Padumuttara Buddha, in the town of Haṃsavatī. And when she was come to years of discretion, she heard the Master preaching, and assigning a certain Bhikkhunī the foremost place in meditative power. Vowing that she would gain that rank, she went on doing good. After aeons upon aeons of rebirth among gods and men, she took birth in this Buddha-epoch in the reigning family of the Sākiyas. Named Nandā, she became known as Beautiful Nandā the Belle of the country. And when our Exalted One had acquired all knowledge, had gone to Kapilavatthu, and caused the princes Nanda and Rāhula to join the Order; when too King Suddhodana died, and the Great Pajāpatī entered the Order, then Nandā thought: 'My elder brother has renounced the heritage of empire, has left the world, and is become a Buddha, a Superman. His son, too, Rāhula, has left the world, so has my brother, King Nanda, my mother, Mahā-Pajāpatī, and my sister, Rāhula's mother. But I now, what shall I do at home ? I will leave the world.' Thus she went forth, not from faith, but from love of her kin. And thus, even after her renunciation, she was intoxicated with her beauty, and would not go into the Master's presence, lest he should rebuke her. But it fared with her even as with Sister Abhirūpa-Nandā, with this difference: When she saw the female shape conjured up by the Master growing gradually aged, her mind, intent on the impermanence and suffering of life, turned to meditative discipline. And the Master, seeing that, taught her suitable doctrine, thus:

Behold, Nandā, the foul compound, diseased,
Impure ! Compel thy heart to contemplate
What is not fair to view.. So steel thyself
And concentrate the well-composed mind. (82)
As with this body, so with thine; as with
Thy beauty, so with this — thus shall it be

With this malodorous, offensive shape,
Wherein the foolish only take delight. (83)
So look thou on it day and night with mind
Unfalteringly steadfast, till alone,
By thine own wit, delivered from the thrall
Of beauty, thou dost gain vision serene. (84)

Then she, heeding the teaching, summoned up wisdom and
stood firm in the fruition of the First Path. And, to give her an
exercise for higher progress, he taught her, saying: 'Nandā, there
is in this body not even the smallest essence. 'Tis but a heap of
bones smeared with flesh and blood under the form of decay and
death.' As it is said in the Dhammapada:

> Have made a citadel of bones besmeared
> With flesh and blood, where ever reign decay
> And death, and where conceit and fraud is stored.

Then she, as he finished, attained Arahantship. And when
she pondered on her victory, she exulted in the Master's words,
and added:

I, even I, have seen, inside and out,
This body as in truth it really is,
Who sought to know the 'what' and 'why' of it,
With zeal unfaltering and ardour fired. (85)
Now for the body care I never more,
And all my consciousness is passion-free.
Keen with unfettered zeal, detached,
Calm and serene I taste Nibbāna's peace. (86)

XLII

Nanduttarā.

She, too, faring in the past as the aforementioned Sisters, was, in this Buddha-age, born in the kingdom of the Kurus at the town of Kammāsadamma, in a brahmin family. And when she had learnt from some of them their arts and sciences, she entered the Order of the Niganthas, and, as a renowned speaker, took her rose-apple bough, like Bhaddā Curlyhair, and toured about the plain of India. Thus she met Mahā-Moggallāna the Elder, and in debate suffered defeat. She thereupon listened to his advice, entered the Order, and not long after attained Arahantship, together with thorough grasp of the letter and meaning of the Norm. And meditating on her victory, she exulted thus:

Fire and the moon, the sun and eke the gods
I once was wont to worship and adore,
Foregathering on the river-banks to go
Down in the waters for the bathing rites. (87)
Ay, manifold observances I laid
Upon me, for I shaved one-half my head,
Nor laid me down to rest save on the earth,
Nor ever broke my fast at close of day. (88)

I sought delight in decking out myself
With gems and ornaments and tricks of art.
By baths, unguents, massage, I ministered
Unto this body, spurred by lusts of sense. (89)

Then found I faith, and forth from home
I went into the homeless life, for I
Had seen the body as it really is,
And nevermore could lusts of sense return. (90)

All the long line of lives were snapt in twain,
Ay, every wish and yearning for it gone.
All that had tied me hand and foot was loosed,
Peace had I won, peace throned in my heart. (91)

XLIII

Mittakālī.

    She, too, faring in the past as the aforementioned Sisters, was, in this Buddha-era, born at the town of Kammāsadamma in the kingdom of the Kurus, in a brahmin's family. Come to years of discretion, she gained faith by hearing the teaching of the great Discourse on the Applications of Mindfulness, and entered the Order of Sisters. For seven years she was liable to a fondness for gifts and honours, and, while doing the duties of a recluse, she was quarrelsome now and again. Later on she was reborn intellectually, and becoming anxious she established insight, and thereupon soon won Arahantship, together with thorough grasp of the Norm in form and in meaning. Reflecting on her victory, she exulted thus:

Leaving my home through call of faith, I sought
The homeless life, and dwelt with eye intent
On offerings from the faithful and the praise
Of this one and the gratitude of that. (92)
The path of insight I neglected, turned
From highest good to follow baser ends.
I lay enthralled to worldly vice, and naught
To win the goal of my high calling wrought. (93)

But anguish crept upon me, even me,
Whenas I pondered in my little cell:
Ah me ! how have I come into this evil road !
Into the power of Craving have I strayed ! (94)
Brief is the span of life yet left to me;
Old age, disease, hang imminent to crush.
Now, ere this body perish and dissolve,
Swift let me be; no time have I for sloth. (95)
And contemplating, as they really are,
The Aggregates of life that come and go,
I rose and stood with mind emancipate !
For me the Buddha's word had come to pass. (96)

XLIV

Sakulā.

Now she, at the time when Padumuttara was Buddha, came
to birth at Haṃsavatī as the daughter of King Ānanda and half-
sister of the Master, and was named Nandā. One day she sat
listening to the master, and hearing him place a Bhikkhunī at the
top of those who had the faculty of the 'Heavenly Eye,' she
vowed that this rank should one day be hers. And after many good
works and subsequent happy rebirths, she came to being on earth
when Kassapa was Buddha, as a brahmin-woman, and renounced
the world as a Wanderer, vowed to a solitary life. One day she
offered her alms at the Master's shrine, making a lamp- offering all
night long. Reborn in the heaven of the Three-and-Thirty Gods,
she became possessed of the Heavenly Eye; and, when this Buddha
was living, she was born a brahmin-woman at Sāvatthī, and called
Pakulā. Assisting at the Master's acceptance of the gift of the Jeta
Grove, she became a believer; and, later on, convinced by the
preaching of an Arahant brother, she grew anxious in mind,

entered the Order, strove and struggled for insight, and soon won Arahantship.

Thereafter, in consequence of her vow, she accumulated skill in the heavenly sight, and was assigned foremost place therein by the Master. And reflecting thereon, thrilled with gladness, she exulted thus:

While yet I dwelt as matron in the house,
I heard a Brother setting forth the Norm.
I saw that Norm, the Pure, the Passionless,
Track to Nibbāna, past decease and birth. (97)
Thereat I left my daughter, left my son,
I left my treasures and my stores of grain;
I called for robes and razors, cut my hair,
And gat me forth into the homeless life. (98)

And first as novice, virtuous and keen
To cultivate the upward mounting Way,
I cast out lust and with it all ill-will,
And therewith, one by one, the deadly Drugs. (99)
Then to the Bhikkhunī of ripening power
Rose in a vision mem'ries of the past.
Limpid and clear the mystic vistas grew,
Expanding by persistent exercise. (100)
Act, speech and thought I saw as not myself,
 Children of cause, fleeting, impermanent.
And now, with every poisonous Drug cast out,
Cool and serene I see Nibbāna's peace. (101)

XLV

Soṇā.

She, too, was born at the time when Padumuttara was Buddha, at Haṃsavatī, in a clansman's family. One day she sat listening to the Master, and hearing him place a Bhikkhunī at the top of those distinguished for capacity of effort, she vowed that this rank should one day be hers. And after many happy rebirths, she came to being, when this Buddha lived, in a clansman's family at Sāvatthī. She became, when married, the mother of ten sons and daughters, and was known as 'the Many-offspringed.' When her husband renounced the world, she set her sons and daughters over the household, handing over all her fortune to her sons, and keeping nothing for herself. Her sons and daughters-in-law had not long supported her before they ceased to show her respect. And saying, 'What have I to do with living in a house where no regard is shown me ?' she entered the Order of Bhikkhunīs. Then she thought: 'I have left the world in my old age; I must work strenuously.' So, while she waited on the Bhikkhunīs, she resolved also to give herself religious studies all night. And she studied thus, steadfast and unfaltering, as one might cling doggedly to a pillar on the veranda, or to a tree in the dark, for fear of hitting one's head against obstacles, never letting go. Thereupon her strenuous energy became known, and the Master, seeing her knowledge maturing, sent forth glory, and appearing as if seated before her, said thus:

> 'The man who, living for an hundred years,
> Beholdeth never the Ambrosial Path,
> Had better live no longer than one day,
> So he behold within that day, that Path !'

And when he had thus spoken, she attained Arahantship. Now, the Exalted One, in assigning rank of merit to the Bhikkhunīs, placed her first for capacity of effort. One day, pondering hereon, she exulted thus:

Ten sons and daughters did I bear within
This heap of visible decay. Then weak
And old I drew near to a Bhikkhunī. (102)
She taught me the Norm, wherein I learnt
The factors, organs, bases of this self,
Impermanent compound. Hearing her words,
And cutting off my hair, I left the world. (103)
Then as I grappled with the threefold course,
Clear shone for my the Eye Celestial.
I know the 'how' and 'when' I came to birth
Down the long past, and where it was I lived. (104)
I cultivate the Signless, and my mind
In uttermost composure concentrate.
Mine is the ecstasy of freedom won
As Path merges in Fruit, and Fruit in Path.
Holding to nought, I in Nibbāna live. (105)
This five-grouped being have I understood.
Cut from its root, all onward growth is stayed.
I too am stayed, victor on basis sure,
Immovable. Rebirth comes never more. (106)

XLVI

Bhaddā Kuṇḍalakesā, the ex-Jain.

She, too, was reborn, when Padumuttara was Buddha, at Haṃsavatī, in a clansman's family. One day she sat listening to the Master, and hearing him place a Bhikkhunī at top of those whose intuition was swift, she vowed that this rank should one day be hers. After working much merit, and experiencing aeons of rebirth among gods and men, she became, when Kassapa was

Buddha, one of the seven daughters of Kiki, King of Kāsī. And for
twenty thousand years she kept the precepts, and built a cell for
the Order. Finally, in this Buddha-era, she was born at Rājagaha,
in the family of the king's treasurer, and called Bhaddā. Growing
up surrounded by attendants, she saw, looking through her lattice,
Satthuka, the chaplain's son, a highwayman, being led to
execution by the city guard by order of the king. Falling in love
with him, she fell prone on her couch saying: 'If I get him, I shall
live; if not, I shall die.' Then her father, hearing of her state, out
of his great love for her, bribed the guard heavily to release the
thief, let him be bathed with perfumed water, adorned him, and let
him come where Bhaddā, decked in jewels, waited upon him. Then
Satthuka very soon coveted her jewels, and said: 'Bhaddā, when
the city guards were taking me to the Robbers' Cliff, I vowed to
the Cliff deity that if my life were spared I would bring an
offering. Do you make one ready.' Wishing to please him, she did
so, and adorning herself with all her jewels, mounted a chariot
with him, and drove to the Cliff. And Satthuka, to have her in his
power, stopped the attendants; and taking the offering, went up
alone with her, but spoke no word of affection to her. And by his
behaviour she discerned his plot. Then he bade her take off her
outer robe and wrap in it the jewels she was wearing. She asked
him what had she done amiss, and he answered: 'You fool, do you
fancy I have come here to make offering ? I have come to get your
ornaments.' 'But whose, then, dear one, are the ornaments, and
whose am I ?' 'I know nothing of that division.' 'So be it, dear;
but grant me this one wish: let me, while wearing my jewels,
embrace you.' He consented, saying: 'Very well.' She thereupon
embraced him in front, and then, as if embracing him from the
back, pushed him over the precipice. And the deity dwelling on the
mountain saw her do this feat and praised her cleverness, saying:

> 'Not in every case is Man the wiser ever;
> Woman, too, when swift to see, may prove as clever.
> Not in every case is Man the wiser reckoned;
> Woman, too, is clever, an she think but a second.'

Thereafter Bhaddā thought: 'I cannot, in this course of events, go home; I will go hence, and leave the world.' So she entered the Order of the Niganṭhas. And they asked her: 'In what grade do you make renunciation ?' 'In whatever is your extreme grade,' she replied, 'perform that on me.' So they tore out her hair with a palmyra comb. (When the hair grew again in close curls they called her Curlyhair.) During her probation she learnt their course of doctrine and concluded that: 'So far as they go they know, but beyond that there is nothing distinctive in their teaching.' So she left them, and going wherever there were learned persons, she learnt their methods of knowledge till, when she found none equal to debate with her, she made a heap of sand at the gate of some village or town, and in it set up the branch of a rose-apple, and told children to watch near it, saying: 'Whoever is able to join issue with me in debate, let him trample on this bough.' Then she went to her dwelling, and if after a week the bough still stood, she took it and departed.

Now at that time our Exalted One, rolling the wheel of the excellent doctrine, came and dwelt in the Jeta Wood near Sāvatthī just when Curlyhair had set up her bough at the gate of that city.

Then the venerable Captain of the Norm (Sāriputta) entered the city alone, and, seeing her bough, felt the wish to tame her. And he asked the children: 'Why is this bough stuck up here ?' They told him. The Elder said: 'If that is so, trample on the bough.' And the children did so. Then Curlyhair, after seeking her meal in the town, came out and saw the trampled bough, and asked who had done it. When she heard it was the Elder, she thought, 'An unsupported debate is not effective,' and going back into Sāvatthī, she walked from street to street, saying: 'Would ye see a debate between the Sākyan recluses and myself ?' Thus, with a great following, she went up to the Captain of the Norm, who was seated beneath a tree, and, after friendly greeting, asked: 'Was it by your orders that my rose-apple bough was trampled on ?' 'Yes, by my orders.' 'That being so, let us have a debate together.' 'Let us, Bhaddā.' 'Which shall put questions, which shall answer ?' 'Questions put to me; do you ask anything you yourself think of.' They proceeded thus, the Elder answering

everything, till she, unable to think of further questions, became
silent. Then the Elder said: 'You have asked much; I, too, will ask,
but only this question.' 'Ask it, lord.' 'One — what is that?'
Curlyhair, seeing neither end nor point to this, was as one gone
into the dark, and said: 'I know not, lord.' Then he, saying, 'You
know not even thus much. How should you know aught else?'
taught her the Norm. She fell at his feet, saying: 'Lord, I take
refuge with you.' 'Come not to me, Bhaddā, for refuge; go for
refuge to the Exalted One, supreme among men and gods.' 'I will
do so, lord,' she said; and that evening, going to the Master at the
hour of his teaching the Norm, and worshipping him she stood on
one side. The Master, discerning the maturity of her knowledge,
said:

> 'Better than a thousand verses, where no profit wings the
> word,
> Is a solitary stanza bringing calm and peace when heard.'

And when he had spoken, she attained Arahantship,
together with thorough grasp of the letter and the spirit. Now she
entered the Order as an Arahant, the Master himself admitting her.
And going to the Sisters' quarters, she abode in the bliss of
fruition and Nibbāna, and exulted in her attainment thus:

Hairless, dirt-laden and half-clad — so fared
I formerly, deeming that harmless things
Held harm, nor was I 'ware of harm
In many things wherein, in sooth, harm lay. (107)
Then forth I went from siesta in the shade
Up to the Vulture's Peak, and there I saw
The Buddha, the Immaculate, begirt
And followed by the Bhikkhu-company. (108)
Low on my knees I worshipped, with both hands
Adoring. 'Come, Bhaddā!' the Master said!
Thereby to me was ordination given. (109)

Lo ! fifty years have I a pilgrim been,
In Anga, Magadha and in Vajjī,
In Kāsī and the land of Kosala,
Nought owing, living on the people's alms. (110)
And great the merit by that layman gained,
Sagacious man, who gave Bhaddā a robe —
Bhaddā who now (captive once more to gear)
Is wholly free from bondage of the mind. (111)

XLVII

Paṭācārā.

She, too, was reborn, when Padumuttara was Buddha, at Haṃsavatī, in a clansman's family. One day she sat listening to the Master, and hearing him place a Bhikkhunī at top of those who were versed in the rules of the Order, she vowed that this rank should one day be hers. After doing good all her life, and being reborn in heaven and on earth, she gained rebirth, in the time when Kassapa was Buddha, as one of the seven Sisters, daughters of Kiki, King of Kāsī. And for 20,000 years she lived a life of righteousness, and built a cell for the Order. While no Buddha lived on earth she dwelt in glory among the gods, and finally, in this Buddha-era, was reborn in the Treasurer's house at Sāvatthī. Grown up, she formed an intimacy with one of the serving-men of her house. When the parents fixed a day on which to give her hand to a youth of her own rank, she took a handful of baggage, and with her lover left the town by the chief gate and dwelt in a hamlet. When the time for her confinement was near, she said: 'Here there's none to take care of me; let us go home, husband.' And he procrastinated, saying: 'We'll go to-day; we'll go to-morrow' till she said; 'The foolish fellow will never take me there'; and setting her affairs in order while he was out, she told her neighbours to say she had gone home, and set forth alone.

When he came back and was told this, he exclaimed: 'Through my doing a lady of rank is without protection,' and hurrying after, overtook her. Midway the pains of birth came upon her, and after she was recovered, they turned back again to the hamlet. At the advent of a second child things happened just as before, with this difference: when midway the winds born of Karma blew upon her, a great storm broke over them, and she said, 'Husband, find me a place out of the rain !' While he was cutting grass and sticks in the jungle, he cut a stake from a tree standing in an ant-hill. And a snake came from the ant-hill and bit him, so that he fell there and died. She, in great misery, and looking for his coming, while the two babies cried at the wind and the rain, placed them in her bosom, and, prone over them on the ground, spent the night thus. At dawn, bearing one babe at her breast, and saying to the other, 'Come, dear, father has left thee,' she went and found him seated, dead, near the ant-heap. 'Oh !' she cried, 'through me my husband is dead,' and wept and lamented all the night. Now, from the rain, the river that lay across her path was swollen knee-deep, and she, being distraught and weak, could not cross the water with both babies. So she left the elder on the hither side, and crossed over with the other. Then she spread out a branch she had broken off, and laid the babe on her rolled headcloth. But she was loth to leave the little creature, and turned round again and again to see him as she went down to the river. Now, when she was half-way over, a hawk in the air took the babe for a piece of flesh, and though the mother, seeing him, clapped her hands, shouting, 'Soo ! soo !' the hawk minded her not, because she was far from him, and caught the child up into the air. Then the elder, thinking the mother was shouting because of him, got flustered, and fell into the river; so she lost both, and came weeping to Sāvatthī. And, meeting a man, she asked him: 'Where do you dwell ?' And he said: 'At Sāvatthī, dame.' 'There is at Sāvatthī such and such a family in such and such a street. Know you them, friend ?' 'I know them, dame; but ask not of them; ask somewhat else.' 'I am not concerned with aught else. 'Tis about them I ask, friend.' 'Dame, can you not take on yourself to tell ? You saw how the god rained all last night ?' 'I saw that, friend. On me he rained all night long. Why, I

will tell you presently. But first, do you tell me of how it goes
with that Treasurer's family.' 'Dame, last night the house broke
down and fell upon them, and they burn the Treasurer, his wife,
and his son on one pyre. Dame, the smoke of it can be seen.'
Thereat grief maddened her, so that she was not aware even of her
clothing slipping off. Wailing in her woe,

> 'My children both are gone, and in the bush
> Dead lies my husband; on one funeral bier
> My mother, father, and my brother burn,'

she wandered around from that day forth in circles, and because her
skirt-cloth fell from her she was given the name 'Cloak-walker.'
And people, seeing her, said: 'Go, little mad-woman !' And some
threw refuse at her head, some sprinkled dust, some pelted her
with clods. The Master, seated in the Jeta Grove, in the midst of a
great company, teaching the Dhamma, saw her wandering thus
round and round, and contemplated the maturity of her knowledge.
When she came towards the Vihāra he also walked that way. The
congregation, seeing her, said: 'Suffer not that little lunatic to
come hither.' The Exalted One said: 'Forbid her not,' and standing
near as she came round again, he said to her: 'Sister, recover thou
presence of mind.' She, by the sheer potency of the Buddha
regaining presence of mind, discerned her undressed plight, and
shame and conscience arising, she fell crouching to earth. A man
threw her his outer robe, and she put it round her, and drawing
near to the Master worshipped at his feet, saying: 'Lord, help me.
One of my children a hawk hath taken, one is borne away by
water; in the jungle my husband lied dead; my parents and my
brother, killed by the overthrown house, burn on one pyre.' So
she told him why she grieved. The Master made her see, thus:
'Paṭācārā, think not thou art come to one able to become a help to
thee. Just as now thou art shedding tears because of the death of
children and the rest, so hast thou, in the unending round of life,
been shedding tears, because of the death of children and the rest,
more abundant than the waters of the four oceans:

'Less are the waters of the oceans four
Than all the waste of waters shed in tears
By heart of man who mourneth touched by Ill.
Why waste thy life brooding in bitter woe ?'

Thus, through the Master's words touching the way where
no salvation lies, the grief in her became lighter to bear. Knowing
this, he went on: 'O Paṭācārā, to one passing to another world no
child not other kin is able to be a shelter or a hiding-place or a
refuge. Not here, even, can they be such. Therefore, let whoso is
wise purify his own conduct, and accomplish the Path leading even
to Nibbāna. Thus he taught her, and said:

'Sons are no shelter, nor father, nor any kinsfolk.
O'ertaken by death, for thee blood-bond is no refuge.
Discerning this truth, the wise man, well ordered by
virtue,
Swiftly makes clear the road leading on to Nibbāna.

When he had finished speaking, she was established in the
fruit of a Stream-winner, and asked for ordination. The Master led
her to the Bhikkhunīs, and let her be admitted.
     She, exercising herself to reach the higher paths, took water
one day in a bowl, and washing her feet, poured away some of the
water, which trickled but a little way and disappeared. She poured
more, and it went farther. And the third time the water went yet
farther before it disappeared. Taking this as her basis of thought,
she pondered: 'Even so do mortals die, either in childhood, or in
middle age, or when old.' And the Master, seated in the 'Fragrant
Chamber,' shed glory around, and appeared as if speaking before
her, saying: 'Even so, O Paṭācārā, are all mortals liable to die;
therefore is it better to have so lived as to see how the five
khandhas come and go, even were it but for one day — ay, but for
one moment — than to live for hundred years and not see that.

'That man who, living for an hundred years,
Beholdeth never how things rise and fall,

Had better live no longer than one day,
So, in that day, he see the flux of things.'

And when he had finished, Paṭācārā won Arahantship,
together with thorough grasp of the Norm in letter and in spirit.
Thereafter, reflecting on how she had attained while yet a student,
and magnifying the advent of this upward change, she exulted
thus:

With ploughshares ploughing up the fields, with seed
Sown in the breast of earth, men with their crops,
Enjoy their gains and nourish wife and child. (112)
Why cannot I, whose life is pure, who seek
To do the Master's will, no sluggard am,
Nor puffed up, win to Nibbāna's bliss ? (113)

One day, bathing my feet, I sit and watch
The water as it trickles down the slope.
Thereby I set my heart in steadfastness,
As one doth train a horse of noble breed. (114)
Then going to my cell, I take my lamp,
And seated on my couch I watch the flame. (115)
Grasping the pin, I pull the wick right down
Into the oil ...
Lo ! the Nibbāna of the little lamp !
Emancipation dawns ! My heart is free ! (116)

XLVIII

Thirty Sisters under Paṭācārā declare their (attainment of) wisdom.

They, too, having made vows under former Buddhas, and accumulating good of age-enduring efficacy in this and that rebirth, consolidated the conditions for emancipation. They came to birth, in this Buddha-dispensation, in clansmen's families in different places, heard Paṭācārā preach, and were by her converted, and entered the Order. To them, perfecting virtue and fulfilling their duties, she one day gave this exhortation:

Men in their prime with pestle and with quern
Are busied pounding rice and grinding corn.
Men in their prime gather and heap up wealth,
To have and nourish wife and children dear. (117)
But ye, my sisters, see ye carry out
The Buddha's will, which bringeth no remorse.
Swiftly bathe ye your feet, then sit ye down
Apart; your souls surrender utterly
To spiritual calm — so do his will. (118)

Then those Bhikkhunīs, abiding in the Sister's admonition, established themselves in insight, performed exercises therein, and brought knowledge to such maturity — the promise, too, being in them — that they attained Arahantship, together with thorough grasp of the Norm in letter and in spirit. And reflecting thereon, they exulted thus, adding the Therī's verses to their own:

The will of her who spake — Paṭācārā —
The thirty Sisters heard and swift obeyed.
Bathing their feet, they sat them down apart,
And gave their souls to spiritual calm,

Fulfilling thus the bidding of the Lord. (119)
While passed the first watch of the night, there rose
Long memories of the bygone line of lives;
While passed the second watch, the Heavenly Eye,
Purview celestial, they clarified;
While passed the last watch of the night, they burst
And rent aside the gloom of ignorance. (120)
Then rising to their feet they hailed her blest:
'Fulfilled is thy will ! and thee we take,
And like to Sakka o'er the thrice ten gods,
Chieftain unconquered in celestial wars,
We place thee as our Chief, and so shall live.
The threefold Wisdom have we gotten now.
From deadly drugs our souls are purified.' (121)

XLIX

Candā.

She, too, faring in former ages like the foregoing, was, in this Buddha-era, born in a brahmin village as the daughter of a brahmin of whom nothing is known. From her childhood her family lost its possessions, and she grew up in wretched circumstances.

Now, in her home the snake-blast disease broke out, and all her kinsfolk caught it, and died. She, being unable to support herself otherwise, went from house to house with a potsherd, maintaining herself by alms. One day she came to where Paṭācārā had just finished her meal. The Bhikkhunīs, seeing her wretched and overcome with hunger, received her with affectionate kindness in the pity they felt for her, and satisfied her with such food as they had. Gladdened by their virtuous conduct, she drew near to the Therī, saluted her, and sat down on one side while the Therī

discoursed. She listened in delight, and, growing anxious
concerning the round of life, renounced the world. Abiding in the
Therī's admonition, she established insight, devoted to practice.
Then, because of her resolve and of the maturity of her
knowledge, she not long after won Arahantship, with thorough
grasp of the Norm in the letter and the spirit. And, reflecting on
her attainment, she exulted thus:

Fallen on evil days was I of yore.
No husband had I, and no child, no friends
Or kin — whence could I food or raiment find ? (122)
As beggars go, I took my bowl and staff,
And sought me alms, begging from house to house,
Sunburnt, frost-bitten, seven weary years. (123)
Then came I where a woman Mendicant
Shared with me food, and drink, and welcomed me,
And said: 'Come forth into our homeless life !' (124)
In gracious pity did she let me come —
Paṭācārā — and heard me take the vows.
And thenceforth words of wisdom and of power
She spake, and set before my face
The way of going to the Crown of Life. (125)
I heard her and I marked, and did her will.
O wise and clear Our Lady's homily !
The Threefold Wisdom have I gotten now.
From deadly drugs my heart is purified. (126)

CANTO VI

PSALMS OF SIX VERSES

L

Paṭācārā's Five Hundred.

These too, having fared under former Buddhas as the
foregoing Sisters, were, in this Buddha-era, reborn in some
clansman's house in divers places, were married, and bore children,
living domestic lives. And having wrought karma such as would
bring to pass such a result, they suffered bereavement in the death
of a child. Then they found their way, overwhelmed with grief, to
Paṭācārā, and saluting her, and seated by her, told her the manner
of their sorrow. The Sister, restraining their sorrow, spake thus:

The way by which men come we cannot know;
Nor can we see the path by which they go.
Why mournest then for him who came to thee,
Lamenting through thy tears: 'My son ! my son !' (127)
Seeing thou knowest not the way he came,
Nor yet the manner of his leaving thee ?
Weep not, for such is here the life of man. (128)
Unask'd he came, unbidden went he hence.
Lo ! ask thyself again whence came thy son
To bide on earth this little breathing space ? (129)
By one way come and by another gone,
As man to die, and pass to other births —
So hither and so hence — why would ye weep ? (130)

They, hearing her doctrine, were filled with agitation, and,
under the Therī, renounced the world. Exercising themselves

henceforth in insight, their faculties growing ripe for
emancipation, they soon became established in Arahantship, with
thorough grasp of the Norm in form and in meaning. Thereafter,
pondering on their attainment, they exulted in those words, 'The
way by which men come,' adding thereto other verses, and
repeating them in turn, as follows:

Lo ! from my heart the hidden shaft is gone,
The shaft that nestled there she hath removed,
And that consuming grief for my dead child
Which poisoned all the life of me is dead. (131)
To-day my heart is healed, my yearning stayed.
Perfected the deliverance wrought in me.
Lo ! I for refuge to the Buddha go —
The only wise — the Order and the Norm. (132)

Now, because those 500 Bhikkhunīs were versed in the
teaching of Paṭācārā, therefore they (all) got the name "Paṭācārā".

LI

Vāsiṭṭhī.

She, too, faring under former Buddhas like the foregoing,
was, in this Buddha- era, reborn in a clansman's family at Vesālī.
Her parents gave her in marriage to a clansman's son of equal
rank, and she, bearing one son, lived happily with her husband.
But when the child was able to run about, he died; and she was
worn and maddened with grief. And while the relatives were
administering healing to the husband, she, unknown to them, ran
away raving, and wandered round and round till she came to
Mithilā. There she saw the Exalted One going down the next
street, self-controlled, self-contained, master of his faculties. And

at the sight of the wondrous Chief, and through the potency of the Buddha, she regained her normal mind from the frenzy that had befallen her. Then the Master taught her the Norm in outline, and in agitation she asked him that she might enter the Order, and by his command she was admitted. Performing all requisite duties and preliminaries, she established insight, and, striving with might and main, and with ripening knowledge, she soon attained Arahantship, together with thorough grasp of the Norm in form and in spirit. Reflecting on her attainment, she exulted thus:

Now here, now there, lightheaded, crazed with grief,
Mourning my child, I wandered up and down,
Naked, unheeding, streaming hair unkempt, (133)
Lodging in scourings of the streets, and where
The dead lay still, and by the chariot-roads —
So three years long I fared, starving, athirst. (134)
And then at last I saw Him, as He went
Within that blessed city Mithilā:
Great Tamer of untamed hearts, yea, Him,
The Very Buddha, Banisher of fear. (135)
Came back my heart to me, my errant mind;
Forthwith to Him I went low worshipping,
And there, e'en at His feet I heard the Norm.
For of His great compassion on us all,
'Twas He who taught me, even Gotama. (136)

I heeded all He said and left the world
And all its cares behind, and gave myself
To follow where He taught, and realize
Life in the Path to great good fortune bound. (137)
Now all my sorrows are hewn down, cast out,
Uprooted, brought to utter end,

In that I now can grasp and understand
The base on which my miseries were built. (138)

LII

Khemā.

Now she, when Padumuttara was Buddha, became a slave
to others, dependent for her livelihood on others, at Haṃsavatī.
And one day, seeing the Elder Sujāta, seeking alms, she gave him
three sweet cakes, and at the same time took down her hair and
gave it to the Elder, saying: 'May I in the future become a disciple,
great in wisdom, of a Buddha !' After many fortunate rebirths as
Queen among both gods and men, for that she had wrought good
karma to the uttermost, she became a human, when Vipassi was
Buddha. Renouncing the world, she became a learned preacher of
the Norm. Reborn, when Kakusandha was Buddha, in a wealthy
family, she made a great park for the Order, and delivered it over to
the Order with the Buddha at their head. She did this again when
Koṇāgamana was Buddha. When Kassapa was Buddha she became
the eldest daughter of King Kiki, named Samaṇī, lived a pious life,
and gave a cell to the Order. Finally, in this Buddha-era, she was
born in Magadha, at Sāgalā, as one of the King's family, and
named Khemā. Beautiful, and with skin like gold, she became the
consort of King Bimbisāra. While the Master was at the Bamboo
Grove she, being infatuated with her own beauty, would not go to
see him, fearing he would look on this as a fault in her. The King
bade persons praise the Grove to her to induce her to visit it. And
accordingly she asked him to let her see it. The King went to the
Vihāra, and seeing no Master, but determined that she should not
get away, he instructed his men to let the Queen see Him of the
Ten Powers, even by constraining her. And this they did when the
Queen was about to leave without meeting the Master. As they
brought her reluctant, the Master, by mystic potency, conjured up
a woman like a celestial nymph, who stood fanning him with a

palmyra leaf. And Khemā, seeing her, thought: 'Verily the Exalted One has around him women as lovely as goddesses. I am not fit even to wait upon such. I am undone by my base and mistaken notions !' Then, as she looked, that woman, through the steadfast will of the Master, passed from youth to middle age and old age, till, with broken teeth, grey hair, and wrinkled skin, she fell to earth with her palm-leaf. Then Khemā, because of her ancient resolve, thought: 'Has such a body come to be a wreck like that ? Then so will my body also !' And the Master, knowing her thoughts, said:

'They who are slaves to lust drift down the stream
Like to a spider gliding down the web
He of himself has wrought. But the released,
Who all their bonds have snapt in twain,
With thoughts elsewhere intent, forsake the world,
And all delight in sense put far away.'

The Commentaries say that when he had finished, she attained Arahantship, together with thorough grasp of the Norm in form and meaning. But according to the Apadāna, she was established only in the Fruit of one who has entered the Stream, and, the King consenting, entered the Order ere she became an Arahant.

Thereafter she became known for her great insight, and was ranked foremost herein by the Exalted One, seated in the conclave of Ariyans at the Jeta Grove Vihāra.

And as she sat one day in siesta under a tree, Māra the Evil One, in youthful shape, drew near, tempting her with sensuous ideas:

'Thou art fair, and life is young, beauteous Khemā !
I am young, even I, too — Come, O fairest lady !
While in our ear fivefold harmonies murmur melodious,
Seek we our pleasure.' (139)

'Through this body vile, foul seat of disease and corruption,
Loathing I feel, and oppression. Cravings of lust are
uprooted. (140)
Lusts of the body and sense-mind cut like daggers and
javelins.
Speak not to me of delighting in aught of sensuous
pleasure !
Verily all such vanities now no more may delight me. (141)
Slain on all sides is the love of the world, the flesh, and the
devil.
Rent asunder the gloom of ignorance once that beset me.
Know this, O Evil One ! Destroyer, know thyself worsted !
(142)

Lo ! ye who blindly worship constellations of heaven,
Ye who fostering fire in cool grove, wait upon Agni,
Ignorant are ye all, ye foolish and young, of the Real,
Deeming ye thus might find purification from evil. (143)

Lo ! as for me I worship th' Enlightened, the Uttermost
Human,
Utterly free from all sorrow, doer of Buddha's
commandments.' (144)

LIII

Sujātā.

   She, too, having made her resolve under former Buddhas,
and accumulating good of age-enduring efficacy in this and that
rebirth, and consolidating the essential conditions for
emancipation, was, in this Buddha-era, reborn at Sāketa, in the

Treasurer's family. Given by her parents in marriage to a Treasurer's son of equal rank, she lived happily with him. Going one day to take part in an Astral Festival in the pleasure-grounds, she was returning with her attendants to the town, when, in the Añjana Grove, she saw the Master, and her heart being drawn to him, she drew near, did obeisance, and seated herself. The Master, finishing his discourse in order, and knowing the sound state of her mind, expounded the Norm to her in an inspiring lesson. Thereat, because her intelligence was fully ripe, she, even as she sat, attained Arahantship, together with thorough grasp of the Norm in form and meaning. Saluting the Master, and going home, she obtained her husband's and her parents' consent, and by command of the Master was admitted to the Order of Bhikkhunīs. Reflecting on her attainment, she exulted thus:

Adorned in finery, in raiment fair,
In garlands wreathed, powdered with sandalwood,
Bedecked with all my jewelry, begirt (145)
With troop of handmaidens, and well-supplied
With food solid and soft, and drink enow,
From home I drove me to the fair pleasaunce. (146)
There did we sport and make a merry time,
Then gat us once more on the homeward way.
So entered we the Grove called Añjana,
Hard by Sāketa, where amidst the trees
Stands the Vihāra (of the holy men). (147)

Him saw I sitting there, Light of the World,
And went into his presence worshipping.
And of his great compassion for us all,
He taught to me the Norm — the One who Sees ! (148)
Forthwith I, too, could pierce and penetrate,
Hearing the truth taught by the mighty Seer,

For there, e'en as I sat, my spirit touched
The Norm Immaculate, th' Ambrosial Path. (149)

Then first it was I left the life of home,
When the blest Gospel I had come to know,
And now the Threefold Wisdom have I won.
O wise and sure the bidding of the Lord ! (150)

LIV

Anopamā.

She, too, having made resolve under former Buddhas, and
heaping up good of age-enduring efficacy in this and that rebirth,
perfecting the conditions tending to bring about emancipation,
was, in this Buddha-era, reborn at Sāketa as the daughter of the
Treasurer, Majjha. Because of her beauty she got the name
'Peerless' (An opamā). When she grew up, many rich men's
sons, Kings' ministers, and Princes, sent messengers to the
father, saying: 'Give us your daughter Anopamā, and we will give
this, or that.' Hearing of this, she — for that the promise of the
highest was in her — thought: 'Profit to me in the life of the
House there is none'; and sought the Master's presence. She heard
him teach, and her intelligence maturing, the memory of that
teaching, and the strenuous effort for insight she made,
established her in the Third Path, that of No-return. Asking the
Master for admission, she was by his order admitted among the
Bhikkhunīs. And on the seventh day thereafter, she realized
Arahantship. Reflecting thereon, she exulted:

Daughter of Treas'rer Majjha's famous house,
Rich, beautiful and prosperous, I was born
To vast possessions and to lofty rank. (151)
Nor lacked I suitors — many came and wooed;

The sons of Kings and merchant princes came
With costly gifts, all eager for my hand.
And messengers were sent from many a land
With promise to my father: 'Give to me (152)
Anopamā, and look ! whate'er she weighs,
Anopamā thy daughter, I will give
Eightfold that weight in gold and gems of price.' (153)

But I had seen th' Enlightened, Chief o' the World,
The One Supreme. In lowliness I sat
And worshipped at his feet. He, Gotama, (154)
Out of his pity taught to me the Norm.
And seated even there I touched in heart
The Anāgāmi-Fruit, Third of the Paths,
And knew this world should see me ne'er return. (155)
Then cutting off the glory of my hair,
I entered on the homeless ways of life.
'Tis now the seventh night since first all sense
Of craving dried up within my heart. (156)

LV

Mahā-Pajāpatī the Gotamid.

Now she was born, when Padumuttara was Buddha, in the
city of Haṃsavatī, in a clansman's family. Hearing the Master
preaching, and assigning the foremost place for experience to a
certain Bhikkhunī, she vowed such a place should one day be hers.
Then, after many births, once more was she reborn in the Buddha-
empty era, between Kassapa and our Buddha, at Benares, as the
forewoman among 500 slave-girls. Now, when the rains drew
near, five Silent Buddhas came down from the Nandamūlaka

mountain-cave to Isipatana, seeking alms; and those women got their husbands to erect five huts for the Buddhas during the three rainy months, and they provided them with all they required during that time. Reborn once more in a weaver's village near Benares, in the headman's family, she again ministered to Silent Buddhas. Finally, she was reborn, shortly before our Master came to us, at Devadaha, in the family of Mahā-Suppabuddha. Her family name was Gotama, and she was the younger sister of the Great Māyā. And the interpreters of birthmarks declared that the children of both sisters would be Wheel-rolling Rulers. Now, King Suddhodana, when he came of age, held a festival, and wedded both the sisters. After this, when our Master had arisen, and, in turing the excellent wheel of the Norm, came in course of fostering souls to Vesālī, his father, who had reached Arahantship, died.

Then the great Pajāpatī, wishing to leave the world, asked the Master for admission, but obtained it not. Then she cut off her hair, put on the robes, and at the end of the sermon now forming the Suttanta on strife and contention, she sallied forth, and together with 500 Sākya ladies whose husbands had renounced the world, went to Vesālī, and asked the Master, through Ānanda the Thera, for ordination. This she then obtained, with the eight maxims for Bhikkhunīs.

Thus ordained, the Great Pajāpatī came and saluted the Master, and stood on one side. Then he taught her the Norm; and she, exercising herself and practising, soon after obtained Arahantship, accompanied by intuitive and analytical knowledge. The remaining 500 Bhikkhunīs, after Nandaka's homily, became endowed with the six branches of intuitive knowledge.

Now, one day, when the Master was seated in the conclave of Ariyans at the great Jeta Grove Vihāra, he assigned the foremost place in experience to Great Pajāpatī, the Gotamid. She, dwelling in the bliss of fruition and of Nibbāna, testified her gratitude one day by declaring her (attainment of) wisdom before the Master, in praising his virtue, who had brought help where before there had been none:

Buddha the Wake, the Hero, hail ! all hail !
Supreme o'er every being that hath life,
Who from all ill and sorrow hast released
Me and so many, many stricken folk. (157)
Now have I understood how Ill doth come.
Craving, the Cause, in me is dried up.
Have I not trod, have I not touched the End
Of Ill — the Ariyan, the Eightfold Path ? (158)

Oh ! but 'tis long I've wandered down all time.
Living as mother, father, brother, son,
And as grandparent in the ages past —
Not knowing how and what things really are.
And never finding what I needed sore. (159)
But now mine eyes have seen th' Exalted One;
And now I know this living frame's the last,
And shattered is th' unending round of births.
No more Pajāpatī shall come to be ! (160)

Behold the company who learn of him,
In happy concord of fraternity,
Of strenuous energy and resolute,
From strength to strength advancing toward the Goal:
The noblest homage this to Buddhas paid. (161)

Oh ! surely for the good of countless lives
Did sister Māyā bring forth Gotama,
Dispeller of the burden of our ill,
Who lay o'erweighted with disease and death ! (162)

LVI

Guttā.

She, too, having made her resolve under former Buddhas, and accumulating good of age-enduring efficacy in this and that rebirth, and consolidating the essential conditions for emancipation, was, in this Buddha-era, reborn at Sāvatthī, in a brahmin's family, and named Guttā. When adolescent, life in the house became repugnant to her, and she obtained her parents' consent to enter the Order under the Great Pajāpatī. Thereafter, though she practised with devotion, her heart long persisted in running after external interests, and this destroyed concentration. Then the Master, to encourage her, sent forth glory, and appeared near her, as if seated in the air, saying these words:

Bethink thee, Guttā, of that high reward
For which thou wast content to lose thy world,
Renouncing hope of children, lure of wealth.
To *that* direct and consecrate the mind,
Nor give thyself to sway of truant thoughts. (163)
Deceivers ever are the thoughts of men,
Fain for the haunts where Māra finds his prey;
And running ever on from birth to birth,
To the dread circle bound — a witless world. (164)
But thou, O Sister, bound to other goals,
Thine is't to break those Fetters five: the lust
Of sense, ill-will, delusion of the Self
The taint of rites and ritual, and doubt, (165)
That drag thee backward to the hither shore.
'Tis not for thee to come again to this ! (166)
Get thee away from life-lust, from conceit,
From ignorance, and from distraction's craze;
Sunder the bonds; so only shalt thou come

To utter end of Ill. Throw off the Chain (167)
Of birth and death — thou knowest what they mean.
So, free from craving, in this life on earth,
Thou shalt go on thy way calm and serene. (168)

And when the Master had made an end of that utterance, the
Sister attained Arahantship, together with thorough grasp of the
Norm in form and meaning. And exulting thereon, she uttered
those lines in their order as spoken by the Exalted One, whence
they came to be called the Therī's psalm.

LVII

Vijayā.

She, too, having made her resolve under former Buddhas,
and heaping up good of age-enduring efficacy, was, in this
Buddha-era, reborn at Rājagaha, in a certain clansman's family.
When grown up she became the companion of Khemā, afterwards
Therī, but then of the laity. Hearing that Khemā had renounced
the world, she said: 'If she, as a King's consort, can leave the
world, surely I can.' So to Khemā Therī she went, and the latter,
discerning whereon her heart was set, taught her the Norm so as
to agitate her mind concerning rebirth, and to make her seek
comfort in the system. And so it came to pass; and the Therī
ordained her. She, serving as was due, and studying as was due,
grew in insight, and, the promise being in her, soon attained to
Arahantship, together with thorough grasp of the Norm and form
and meaning. And she, reflecting thereon, exulted thus:

Four times, nay five, I sallied from my cell,
And roamed afield to find the peace of mind
I lacked, and governance of thoughts
I could not bring into captivity. (169)

Then to a Bhikkhunī I came and asked
Full many a question of my doubts.
To me she taught the Norm: the elements,   (170)
Organ and object in the life of sense,
[And then the factors of the Nobler life:]
The Ariyan Truths, the Faculties, the Powers,
The Seven Features of Awakening,
The Eightfold Way, leading to utmost good. (171)
I heard her words, her bidding I obeyed.
While passed the first watch of the night there rose
Long memories of the bygone line of lives. (172)
While passed the second watch, the Heavenly Eye,
Purview celestial, I clarified.
While passed the last watch of the night, I burst
And rent aside the gloom of ignorance. (173)
Then, letting joy and blissful ease of mind
Suffuse my body, seven days I sat,
Ere stretching out cramped limbs I rose again.
Was it not rent indeed, that muffling mist ? (174)

CANTO VII

PSALMS OF SEVEN VERSES

LVIII

Uttarā.

She, too, having made her resolve under former Buddhas, and heaping up good of age-enduring efficacy in this and that rebirth, so that in her the root of good (karma) was well planted, and the requisites for emancipation were well stored up, was, in this Buddha-era, reborn at Sāvatthī, in a certain clansman's family, and called Uttarā. Come to years of discretion, she heard Paṭācārā preach the Norm, became thereby a believer, entered the Order, and became an Arahant. And, reflecting on her attainment, she exulted thus:

'Men in their prime, with pestle and with quern
Are busied pounding rice and grinding corn.
Men in their prime gather and heap up wealth,
To have and nourish wife and children dear. (175)
Yours is the task to spend yourselves upon
The Buddha's will which bringeth no remorse.
Swiftly bathe ye your feet, then sit ye down (176)
Apart. Planting your minds in Steadfastness,
With concentrated effort well composed,
Ponder how what ye do, and say, and think,
Proceeds not from a Self, is not your Self. (177)
The will of her who spake — Paṭācārā —
I heard and marked and forthwith carried out.
Bathing my feet, I sat me down apart. (178)
While passed the first watch of the night there rose

Long memories of the bygone line of lives.
While passed the second watch, the Heavenly Eye,
Purview celestial, I clarified. (179)
While passed the third watch of the night, I burst
And rent aside the gloom of ignorance.

Now rich in Threefold Wisdom I arose:
'O Lady ! verily thy will is done. (180)
And like to Sakka o'er the thrice ten gods,
Chieftain unconquered in celestial wars,
I place thee as my chief, and so shall live.
The Threefold Wisdom have I gotten now.
From deadly drugs my soul is purified. (181)

Now this Sister, one day, when under Paṭācārā she had
established herself in an exercise, went into her own dwelling, and
seated herself cross-legged, thought: 'I will not break up this
sitting until I have emancipated my heart from all dependence on
the Āsavas.' Thus resolving, she incited her intellectual grasp, and
gradually clarifying insight as she progressed along the Paths, she
attained Arahantship, together with the power of intuition and
thorough grasp of the Norm. Thus contemplating nineteen
subjects in succession, with the consciousness that 'Now have I
done what herein I had to do,' she uttered in her happiness the
verses given above, and stretched her limbs. And when the dawn
arose, and night brightened into day, she sought the Therī's
presence, and repeated her verses.

LIX

Cālā.

She, too, having made her resolve under former Buddhas, and heaping up good of age-enduring efficacy in subsequent rebirths, was, in this Buddha-era, reborn in Magadha, at the village of Nālaka, the child of Surūpasārī, the Brahmin-woman. And on her name-giving day they called her Cālā. Her younger sister was Upacālā, and the youngest Sīsūpacālā, and all three were junior to their brother Sāriputta, Captain of the Norm. Now, when the three heard that their brother had left the world for the Order, they said: 'This can be no ordinary system, nor ordinary renunciation, if one like our brother have followed it !'. And full of desire and longing, they too renounced the world, putting aside their weeping kinsfolk and attendants. Thereupon, with striving and endeavour, they attained Arahantship, and abode in the bliss of Nibbāna.

Now, Cālā Bhikkhunī, after her round and her meal, entered one day the Dark Grove to take siesta. Then Māra came to stir up some sensual desires in her. Is it not told in the Sutta ?

Again, Cālā Bhikkhunī, after her round in Sāvatthī and her meal, entered one day the Pleasant Grove for siesta. And, going on down into the Dark Grove, she sat down under a tree. Then Māra came, and, wishing to upset the consistency of her religious life, asked her the questions in her Psalm. When she had expounded to him the virtues of the Master, and the guiding power of the Norm, she showed him how, by her own attained proficiency, he was exceeding his tether. Thereat Māra, dejected and melancholy, vanished. But she discoursed in exultation on what both of them had said, as follows:

Lo here ! a Sister who the fivefold sense
Of higher life hath trained and, self-possessed,
Herself well held in hand, hath made her way
Where lies the Holy Path, where dwells the Bliss

Of mastery over action, speech and thought. (182)

Māra

Why now and whereto art thou seen thus garbed
And shaven like a nun, yet dost not join
Ascetics of some sect, and share their rites ?
What, futile and infatuate, is thy quest ? (183)

Cālā

'Tis they that are without, caught in the net
Of the vain shibboleths on which they lean —
'Tis they that have no knowledge of the Truth,
'Tis they that lack all competence therein. (184)

Lo ! in the princely Sākiya clan is born
A Buddha, peerless 'mong the sons of men:
'Tis he hath shown the saving Truth to me
Which vain opinions doth overpass, (185)
Even the What and Why of Ill, and how
Ill comes, and how Ill may be overpassed,
E'en by the Ariyan, the Eightfold Path,
That leadeth to th' abating of all Ill. (186)
And I who heard his blessed words abide
Fain only and alway to do his will.
The Threefold Wisdom have I gotten now,
And done the bidding of the Buddha blest. (187)
On every hand the love of sense is slain.
And the thick gloom of ignorance is rent

In twain. Know this, thou Evil One, avaunt !
Here, O Destroyer ! shalt thou not prevail. (188)

LX

Upacālā.

Her story has been told in the foregoing number. Like Cālā, she, too, as Arahant, exulted, after Māra had tempted her in vain, as follows:

Lo ! here a Sister who the fivefold sense
Of higher life hath trained, with memory
And power of inward vision perfected,
And thus hath made her way into the Path
Of Holiness, by noble spirits trod. (189)

Māra

Why lovest thou not birth ? since, being born,
Thou canst enjoy what life of sense doth bring.
Enjoy the sport of sense and take thy fill,
Lest thou too late with bitter pangs regret. (190)

Upacālā

To one that's born death cometh soon or late.
And many perils at the hands of men:
Scathe, torture, loss of limb, of liberty.
Nay, life. So Ill-ward bound is the born child. (191)
Lo ! in the princely Sākiya clan is born
He who is Wholly Wake, Invincible.

'Tis he hath shown the saving Truth to me
By which the round of birth is overpassed, (192)
E'en the What and Why of Ill, and how
Ill comes, and how Ill may be overpassed,
E'en by the Ariyan, the Eightfold Path,
That leadeth to th' abating of all Ill. (193)

And I who heard his blessed words, abide
Fain only and alway to do his will.
The Threefold Wisdom have I gotten now,
And done the bidding of the Buddha blest. (194)
On every hand the love of sense is slain.
And the thick gloom of ignorance is rent
In twain. Know this, thou Evil One, avaunt !
Here, O Destroyer ! may'st thou not prevail. (195)

CANTO VIII

PSALM OF EIGHT VERSES

LXI

Sīsupacālā.

Her story has been told in that of Cālā her sister — how she followed in her great brother's steps, entered the Order, and became an Arahant. Dwelling in the bliss of fruition, she reflected one day on her attainment, and having done all that was to be done, exulted in her happiness thus:

Lo ! here a Sister, in the Precepts sure,
Well-guarded in the sixfold way of sense,
Who hath attained to that Holy Path,
That ever-welling elixir of life. (196)

Māra

Now think upon the Three-and-Thirty Gods,
And on the gods who rule in realm of Shades,
On those who reign in heaven of Bliss, and on
Those higher deities who live where life
Yet flows by way of sense and of desire:
Think and thither aspire with longing heart,
Where in past ages thou hast lived before. (197)

When the Therī heard, she said: 'Stop, Māra ! the Kāmaloka of which you talk is, even as is the whole of the world, burning and blazing with the fires of lust, hate, and ignorance. 'Tis not there the discerning mind can find any charm.' And

showing Māra how her mind was turned away from the world and
from desires of sense, she upbraided him thus:

Ay, think upon the Three-and-Thirty gods.
And on the gods who rule in realm of Shades;
On those who reign in heaven of Bliss, and on
Those higher deities who live where life
Yet flows by way of sense and of desire. (198)
Consider how time after time they go
From birth to death, and death to birth again,
Becoming this and then becoming that,
Ever beset by the recurring doom
Of hapless individuality,
Whence comes no merciful enfranchisement. (199)

On fire is all the world, is all in flames !
Ablaze is all the world, the heav'ns do quake ! (200)
But that which quaketh not, that ever sure,
That priceless thing, unheeded by the world,
Even the Norm — that hath the Buddha taught
To me, therein my mind delighted dwells. (201)
And I who heard his blessed word abide
Fain only and alway to do his will.
The Threefold Wisdom have I gotten now,
And done the bidding of the Buddha blest. (202)
On every hand the love of sense is slain
And the thick gloom of ignorance is rent
In twain. Know this, O Evil One, avaunt !
Here, O Destroyer, shalt thou not prevail ! (203)

CANTO IX

LXII

Vaḍḍha's Mother.

She, too, having made her resolve under former Buddhas, and heaping up good of age-enduring efficacy in this and that rebirth, till the preparation for achieving emancipation was gradually become perfect, was, in this Buddha-era, reborn at the town of Bhārukaccha, in a clansman's family. When married, she bore one son, and he was given the name Vaḍḍha. From that time she was known as Vaḍḍha's mother. Hearing a Bhikkhu preach, she became a believer, and, handing her child over to her kin, she went to the Bhikkhunīs, and entered the Order. The rest, not told here, may be filled in from Brother Vaḍḍha's story told in the Psalms of the Elder Brethren. Vaḍḍha, to see his mother, went alone into and through the Bhikkhunīs' quarters; and she, saying, 'Why have you come in here alone?' admonished him as follows:

O nevermore, my Vaḍḍha, do thou stray
Into the jungle of this world's desires.
Child of my heart ! come thou not back and forth
To share, reborn, in all the ills of life. (204)
True happiness, O Vaḍḍha mine, is theirs
Who, wise and freed from longing and from doubt,
Cool and serene, have tamed the craving will,
And dwell immune from all the deadly drugs. (205)
The Way that Sages such as these have trod —
Leading to that pure vision how they may
Make a sure end of Ill — do thou, dear lad,
Study and cause to grow to thine own weal. (206)

And Vaddha, thinking, 'My mother is surely established in Arahantship', expressed himself thus:

Now in good hope and faith thou speakest thus,
O little mother ! well I trow, for thee.
Dear mother mine, no jungle bars the way. (207)

Then the Therī replied, showing her work was done:

Ah, no ! my Vaddha, whatsoe'er I do
Or say, or think, in things or great or small,
Not e'en the smallest growth of jungly vice
Yet standeth in the onward way for me. (208)
For all the deadly poison-plants are killed
In me who meditate with strenuous zeal.
The Threefold Wisdom have I gotten now,
And all the Buddha's word have I fulfilled. (209)

The Brother, using her exhortation as a goad, and stimulated thereby, went to his Vihāra, and, seated in his wonted resting-place, so made insight to grow that he attained Arahantship. And reflecting in happiness on his attainment, he went to his mother, and declared his (attainment of) wisdom:

O splendid was the spur my mother used,
And no less merciful the chastisement
She gave to me, even the rune she spoke,
Fraught with its burden of sublimest good. (210)
I heard her words, I marked her counsel wise,
And thrilled with righteous awe as she called up
The vision of salvation to be won. (211)

And night and day I strove unweariedly
Until her admonitions bore their fruit,
And I could touch Nibbāna's utter peace. (212)

CANTO X

LXIII

Kisā-Gotamī.

Now she was born, when Padumuttara was Buddha, in the city of Haṃsavatī, in a clansman's family. And one day she heard the Master preach the Dhamma, and assign foremost rank to a Bhikkhunī with respect to the wearing of rough garments. She vowed that this rank should one day be hers. In this Buddha-era she was reborn at Sāvatthī, in a poor family. Gotamī was her name, and from the leanness of her body she was called Lean Gotamī. And she was disdainfully treated when married, and was called a nobody's daughter. But when she bore a son, they paid her honour. Then, when he was old enough to run about and play, he died, and she was distraught with grief. And, mindful of the change in folk's treatment of her since his birth, she thought: 'They will even try to take my child and expose him.' So, taking the corpse upon her hip, she went, crazy with sorrow, from door to door, saying: 'Give me medicine for my child !' And people said with contempt: 'Medicine ! What's the use ?' She understood them not. But one sagacious person thought: 'Her mind is upset with grief for her child. He of the Tenfold Power will know of some medicine for her.' And he said: 'Dear woman, go to the Very Buddha, and ask him for medicine to give your child.' She went to the Vihāra at the time when the Master taught the Doctrine, and said: 'Exalted One, give me medicine for my child !' The Master, seeing the promise in her, said: 'Go, enter the town, and at any house where yet no man hath died, thence bring a little mustard-seed.' ''Tis well, lord !' she said, with mind relieved; and, going to the first house in the town, said: 'Let me take a little mustard, that I may give medicine to my child. If in this house no man hath yet died, give me a little mustard.' 'Who may say how many have not died here ?' 'With such mustard, then, I have nought to do.' So she went on to the second and a third house, until, by the might of the Buddha, her frenzy left her, her natural mind was restored, and she thought: 'Even this will be the order of things in the whole town. The Exalted One foresaw this out of his pity for my good.' And, thrilled at the thought, she left the town and laid her child in the charnel-field, saying:

> 'No village law is this, no city law,
> No law for this clan, or for that alone;
> For the whole world — ay, and the gods in heav'n —
> This is the Law: All is impermanent !'

So saying, she went to the Master. And he said: 'Gotamī, hast thou gotten the little mustard ?' And she said: 'Wrought is the work, lord, of the little mustard. Give thou me confirmation.' Then the Master spoke thus:

> 'To him whose heart on children and on goods
> Is centred, cleaving to them in his thoughts,
> Death cometh like a great flood in the night,
> Bearing away the village in its sleep.'

When he had spoken, she was confirmed in the fruition of the First (the Stream-entry) Path, and asked for ordination. He consented, and she, thrice saluting by the right, went to the Bhikkhunīs, and was ordained. And not long afterwards, studying the causes of things, she caused her insight to grow. Then the Master said a Glory-verse:

> 'The man who, living for an hundred years,
> Beholdeth never the Ambrosial Path,
> Had better live no longer than one day,
> So he behold within that day the Path.'

When he had finished, she attained Arahantship. And becoming pre-eminent in ascetic habits, she was wont to wear

raiment of triple roughness. Then the Master, seated in the Jeta
Grove in conclave, and assigning rank of merit to the Bhikkhunīs,
proclaimed her first among the wearers of rough raiment. And she,
reflecting on what great things she had won, uttered this Psalm
before the Master, in praise of friendship with the elect:

Friendship with noble souls throughout the world
The Sage hath praised. A fool, in sooth, grows wise
If he but entertain a noble friend. (213)
Cleave to the men of worth ! In them who cleave
Wisdom doth grow; and in that pious love
From all your sorrows shall ye be released. (214)

Mark Sorrow well; mark ye how it doth come,
And how it passes; mark the Eightfold path
That endeth woe, the Four great Ariyan Truths. (215)
Woeful is woman's lot ! hath he declared,
Tamer and Driver of the hearts of men:
Woeful when sharing home with hostile wives,
Woeful when giving birth in bitter pain,
Some seeking death, or e'er they suffer twice, (216)
Piercing the throat; the delicate poison take,
Woe too when mother-murdering embryo
Comes not to birth, and both alike find death. (217)

'Returning home to give birth to my child,
I saw my husband in the jungle die.
Nor could I reach my kin ere travail came. (218)
My baby boys I lost, my husband too.
And when in misery I reached my home,
Lo ! where together on a scanty pyre,
My mother, father, and my brother burn !' (219)

O wretched, ruined woman ! all this weight
Of sorrows hast thou suffered, shed these tears
Through weary round of many thousand lives. (220)
I too have seen where, in the charnel-field,
Devoured was my baby's tender flesh.

Yet she, her people slain, herself outcast,
Her husband dead, hath thither come
Where death is not ! (221)
Lo! I have gone
Up on the Ariyan, on the Eightfold Path
That goeth to the state ambrosial.
Nibbāna have I realized, and gazed
Into the Mirror of the holy Norm. (222)
I, even I, am healed of my hurt,
Low is my burden laid, my task is done,
My heart is wholly set at liberty.
I, sister Kisā-Gotamī, have uttered this ! (223)

CANTO XI

PSALM OF TWELVE VERSES

LXIV

Uppalavaṇṇā.

She, too, was born, when Padumuttara was Buddha, at the city Haṃsavatī, in a clansman's family. And when grown up she heard, with a great multitude, the Master teach, and assign a certain Bhikkhunī the chief place among those who had mystic potency. And she gave great gifts for seven days to the Buddha and the Order, and aspired to that same rank ...

In this Buddha-age, she was reborn at Sāvatthī as the daughter of the Treasurer. And because her skin was of the colour of the heart of the blue lotus, they called her Uppalavaṇṇā. Now, when she was come of age, kings and commoners from the whole of India sent messengers to her father, saying: 'Give us your daughter.' Thereupon the Treasurer thought: 'I cannot possibly meet the wishes of all. I will devise a plan.' And, sending for his daughter, he said: 'Dear one, are you able to leave the world ?' To her, because she was in her final stage of life, his words were as if oil a hundred times refined had anointed her head. Therefore she said: 'Dear father, I will renounce the world !' He, honouring her, brought her to the Bhikkhunīs' quarters, and let her be ordained.

A little while afterwards it became her turn for office in the house of the Sabbath. And, lighting the lamp, she swept the room. Then taking the flame of the lamp as a visible sign, and contemplating it continually, she brought about Jhāna by way of the Lambent Artifice, and making that her stepping-stone, she attained Arahantship. With its fruition, intuition and grasp of the Norm were achieved, and she became especially versed in the mystic potency of transformation.

And the Master, seated in conclave in the Jeta Grove, assigned her the foremost rank in the mystic powers. She,

pondering the bliss of Jhāna and of fruition, repeated one day
certain verses. They had been uttered in anguish by a mother who
had been living as her daughter's rival with him who later, when a
Bhikkhu, became known as the Ganges-bank Elder, and were a
reflection on the harm, the vileness and corruption of sensual
desires:

I

'In enmity we lived, bound to one man,
Mother and daughter, both as rival wives !
O what a woeful plight, I found, was ours,
Unnatural offence ! My hair stood up. (224)
Horror fell on me. Fie upon this life
Of sensual desire, impure and foul,
A jungle thick with thorny brake, wherein
We hapless pair, my girl and I, had strayed !' (225)
The evils in the life of sense, the strong
Sure refuge in renouncing all, she saw.
At Rājagaha went she forth and left
The home to live the life where no home is. (226)

II

  Joyful and happy, she meditates on the distinction she has
won:

How erst I lived I know; the Heavenly Eye,
Purview celestial, have I clarified;
Clear too the inward life that others lead;
Clear too I hear the sounds ineffable; (227)
Powers supernormal have I made mine own;
And won immunity from deadly Drugs.

These, the six higher knowledges are mine.
Accomplished is the bidding of the Lord. (228)

III

     She works a marvel before the Buddha with his consent, and records the same:

With chariot and horses four I came,
Made visible by supernormal power,
And worshipped, wonder working, at his feet,
The wondrous Buddha, Sovran of the world. (229)

IV

     She is disturbed by Māra in the Sāl-tree Grove, and rebukes him:

Māra

Thou that art come where fragrant the trees stand crowned with blossoms,
Standest alone in the shade, maiden so [fair and] foolhardy,
None to companion thee — fearest thou not the wiles of seducers ? (230)

She

Were there an hundred thousand seducers e'en such as thou art,
Ne'er would a hair of me stiffen or tremble — alone what canst thou do ? (231)

Here though I stand, I can vanish and enter into thy body.
See ! I stand 'twixt thine eyebrows, stand where thou canst
not see me. (232)

For all my mind is wholly self-controlled,
And the four Paths to Potency are throughly learnt,
Yea, the six Higher Knowledges are mine.
Accomplished is the bidding of the Lord. (233)

Like spears and jav'lins are the joys of sense,
That pierce and rend the mortal frames of us.
These that thou speak'st of as the joys of life —
Joys of that ilk to me are nothing worth. (234)
On every hand the love of pleasure yields,
And the thick gloom of ignorance is rent
In twain. Know this, O Evil One, avaunt !
Here, O Destroyer ! shalt thou not prevail. (235)

CANTO XII

PSALM OF SIXTEEN VERSES

LXV

Puṇṇā or Puṇṇikā.

She, too, having made her resolve under former Buddhas, and heaping up good of age-enduring efficacy in this and that rebirth, was, when Vipassi was Buddha, reborn in a clansman's family. Come to years of discretion, because of the promise that was in her, she waxed anxious at the prospect of rebirth, and, going to the Bhikkhunīs, heard the Norm, believed, and entered the Order. Perfect in virtue, and learning the Three Piṭakas, she became very learned in the Norm, and a teacher of it. The same destiny befell her under the five succeeding Buddhas — Sikhi, Vessabhu, Kakusandha, Koṇāgamana, and Kassapa. But because of her tendency to pride, she was unable to root out the defilements. So it came to pass, through the karma of her pride, that, in this Buddha-era, she was reborn at Sāvatthī, in the household of Anāthapiṇḍika, the Treasurer, of a domestic slave. She became a Stream-entrant after hearing the discourse of the Lion's Roar. Afterwards, when she had converted (lit. tamed) the baptist brahmin, and so won her master's esteem that he made her a freed woman, she obtained his consent, as her guardian and head of her home, to enter the Order. And, practising insight, she in no long time won Arahantship, together with thorough grasp of the Norm in form and in meaning. Reflecting on her attainment, she uttered these verses in exultation:

Drawer of water, I down to the stream,
Even in winter, went in fear of blows,
Harassed by fear of blame from mistresses. (236)

'What, brahmin, fearest thou that ever thus
Thou goest down into the river ? Why
With shiv'ring limbs dost suffer bitter cold ?' (237)

'Well know'st thou, damsel Puṇṇikā, why ask
One who by righteous karma thus annuls
Effect of evil karma ? Who in youth, (238)
Or age ill deeds hath wrought, by baptism
Of water from that karma is released.' (239)

'Nay now, who, ignorant to the ignorant,
Hath told thee this; that water-baptism
From evil karma can avail to free ? (240)
Why then the fishes and the tortoises,
The frogs, the watersnakes, the crocodiles
And all that haunt the water straight to heaven (241)
Will go. Yea, all who evil karma work —
Butchers of sheep and swine, fishers, hunters of game,
Thieves, murders — so they but splash themselves
With water, are from evil karma free ! (242)
And if these streams could bear away what erst
Of evil thou hast wrought, they'd bear away
Thy merit too, leaving thee stripped and bare. (243)
That, dreading which, thou, brahmin, comest e'er
To bathe and shiver here, that, even that
Leave thou undone, and save thy skin from frost.' (244)

'Men who in error's ways had gone aside
Thou leadest now into the Ariyan Path.
Damsel, my bathing raiment give I thee.' (245)

'Keep thou thy raiment ! Raiment seek I none.
If ill thou fearest, if thou like it not, (246)
Do thou no open, nor no hidden wrong.
But if thou shalt do evil, or hast done, (247)
Then is there no escape for thee from ill,
E'en tho' thou see it come, and flee away.
If thou fear ill, if ill delight thee not, (248)
Go thou and seek the Buddha and the Norm
And Order for thy refuge; learn of them
To keep the Precepts. Thus shalt thou find good.' (249)

'Lo ! to the Buddha I for refuge go,
And to the Norm and Order. I will learn
Of them to take upon myself and keep
The Precepts; so shall I indeed find good. (250)

Once but a son of brahmins born was I,
To-day I stand brahmin in very deed.
The nobler Threefold Wisdom have I won,
Won the true Veda-lore, and graduate
Am I, from better Sacrament returned,
Cleansed by the inward spiritual bath. (251)

For the brahmin, established in the Refuges and the
Precepts, when later he had heard the Master preach the Norm,
became a believer and entered the Order. Using every effort, he not
long after became Thrice-Wise, and, reflecting on his state,
exulted in those verses. And the Sister, repeating them of herself,
they all became her Psalm.

CANTO XIII

PSALMS OF ABOUT TWENTY VERSES

LXVI

Ambapālī.

She, too, having made her resolve under former Buddhas, and heaping up good of age-enduring efficacy in this or that rebirth, entered the Order when Sikhi was Buddha. And one day, while yet a novice, she was walking in procession with Bhikkhunīs, doing homage at a shrine, when an Arahant Therī in front of her hastily spat in the court of the shrine. Coming after her, but not having noticed the Therī's action, she said in reproof: 'What prostitute has been spitting in this place ?'

As a Bhikkhunī, observing the Precepts, she felt repugnance for rebirth by parentage, and set her mind intently on spontaneous re-generation. So in her last birth she came into being spontaneously at Vesālī, in the King's gardens, at the foot of a mango-tree. The gardener found her, and brought her to the city. She was known as the Mango-guardian's girl. And such was her beauty, grace, and charm that many young Princes strove with each other to possess her, till, in order to end their strife, and because the power of karma impelled them, they agreed to appoint her courtesan. Later on, out of faith in the Master, she built a Vihāra in her own gardens, and handed it over to him and the Order. And when she had heard her own son, the Elder Vimala-Kondañña, preach the Norm, she worked for insight, and studying the law of impermanence as illustrated in her own ageing body, she uttered the following verses:

Glossy and black as the down of the bee my curls once clustered.

They with the waste of the years are liker to hempen or bark cloth.

Such and not otherwise runneth the rune, the word of the Soothsayer. (252)

Fragrant as casket of perfumes, as full of sweet blossoms the hair of me.

All with the waste of the years now rank as the odour of hare's fur.

Such and not otherwise runneth the rune, the word of the Soothsayer. (253)

Dense as a grove well planted, and comely with comb, pin, and parting.

All with the waste of the years dishevelled the fair plaits and fallen.

Such and not otherwise runneth the rune, the word of the Soothsayer. (254)

Glittered the swarthy plaits in head-dresses jewelled and golden.

All with the waste of the years broken, and shorn are the tresses.

Such and not otherwise runneth the rune, the word of the Soothsayer. (255)

Wrought as by sculptor's craft the brows of me shone,
finely pencilled.
They with the waste of the years are seamèd with wrinkles,
o'erhanging.
Such and not otherwise runneth the rune, the word of the
Soothsayer. (256)

Flashing and brilliant as jewels, dark-blue and long-lidded the
eyes of me.
They with the waste of the years spoilt utterly, radiant no
longer.
Such and not otherwise runneth the rune, the word of the
Soothsayer. (257)

Dainty and smooth the curve of the nostrils e'en as in
children.
Now with the waste of years searèd the nose is and
shrivelled.
Such and not otherwise runneth the rune, the word of the
Soothsayer. (258)

Lovely the lines of my ears as the delicate work of the
goldsmith.
They with the waste of the years are seamèd with wrinkles
and pendent.
Such and not otherwise runneth the rune, the word of the
Soothsayer. (259)

Gleamed as I smiled my teeth like the opening buds of the plantain.
They with the waste of the years are broken and yellow as barley.
So and not otherwise runneth the rune, the word of the Soothsayer. (260)

Sweet was my voice as the bell of the cuckoo through woodlands flitting.
Now with the waste of the years broken the music and halting.
So and not otherwise runneth the rune, the word of the Soothsayer. (261)

Softly glistened of yore as mother-of-pearl the throat of me.
Now with the waste of the years all wilted its beauty and twisted.
So and not otherwise runneth the rune, the word of the Soothsayer. (262)

Beauteous the arms of me once shone like twin pillars cylindrical.
They with the waste of the years hang feeble as withering branches.
So and not otherwise runneth the rune, the word of the Soothsayer. (263)

Beauteous of yore were my soft hands with rings and gewgaws resplendent.
They with the waste of the years like roots are knotted and scabrous.

So and not otherwise runneth the rune, the word of the Soothsayer. (264)

Full and lovely in contour rose of yore the small breasts of me.
They with the waste of the years droop shrunken as skins without water.
So and not otherwise runneth the rune, the word of the Soothsayer. (265)

Shone of yore this body as shield of gold well-polishèd.
Now with the waste of the years all covered with network of wrinkles.
So and not otherwise runneth the rune, the word of the Soothsayer. (266)

Like to the coils of a snake the full beauty of yore of the thighs of me.
They with the waste of the years are even as stems of the bamboo.
So and not otherwise runneth the rune, the word of the Soothsayer. (267)

Beauteous to see were my ankles of yore, bedecked with gold bangles.
They with the waste of the years are shrunken as faggots of sesamum.
So and not otherwise runneth the rune, the word of the Soothsayer. (268)

Soft and lovely of yore as though filled out with down were
the feet of me.
They with the waste of the years are cracked open and
wizened with wrinkles.
So and not otherwise runneth the rune, the word of the
Soothsayer. (269)

Such hath this body been. Now age-weary and weak and
unsightly,
Home of manifold ills; old house whence the mortar is
dropping.
So and not otherwise runneth the rune, the word of the
Soothsayer. (270)

And inasmuch as the Therī, by the visible signs of
impermanence in her own person, discerned impermanence in all
phenomena of the three planes, and bearing that in mind, brought
into relief the signs of Ill and of Not-Self, she, making clear her
insight in her Path-progress, attained Arahantship.

LXVII

Rohiṇī.

She, too, having made her resolve under former Buddhas,
and heaping up good of age-enduring efficacy in this and that
rebirth, was born, ninety-one aeons ago, in the time of Vipassi
Buddha, in a clansman's family. One day she saw the Exalted One
seeking alms in the city of Bandhumatī, and filling his bowl with
sweet cakes, she worshipped low at his feet in joy and gladness.
And when, after many rebirths in heaven and on earth in
consequence thereof, she had accumulated the conditions requisite
for emancipation, she was, in this Buddha-era, reborn at Vesālī in

the house of a very prosperous brahmin, and named Rohiṇī. Come to years of discretion, she went, while the Master was staying at Vesālī, to the Vihāra, and heard the doctrine. She became a 'Stream-entrant,' and teaching her parents the doctrine, and they accepting it, she gained their leave to enter the order. Studying for insight, she not long after attained Arahantship, together with thorough grasp of the Norm in form and meaning.

And reflecting on a discussion she had had with her father while she had yet only entered the Stream, she uttered the substance of it as verses of exultation:

'"See the recluses !" dost thou ever say.
"See the recluses !" waking me from sleep.
Praise of recluses ever on thy tongue.
Say, damsel, hast a mind recluse to be ? (271)
Thou givest these recluses as they come,
Abundant food and drink. Come, Rohiṇī.
I ask, why are recluses dear to thee ? (272)
Not fain to work are they, the lazy crew.
They make their living off what others give.
Cadging are they, and greedy of tit-bits —
I ask, why are recluses dear to thee ? (273)

Full many a day, dear father, hast thou asked
Touching recluses. Now will I proclaim
Their virtues and their wisdom and their work. (274)

Full fain of work are they, no sluggard crew.
The noblest work they do; they drive out lust
And hate. Hence are recluses dear to me. (275)

The three fell roots of evil they eject,
Making all pure within, leaving no smirch,

No stain. Hence are recluses dear to me. (276)

Their work in action's pure, pure is their work
In speech, and pure no less than these their work
In thought. Hence are recluses dear to me. (277)

Immaculate as seashell or as pearl,
Of lustrous characters compact, without,
Within. Hence are recluses dear to me. (278)

Learn'd and proficient in the Norm; elect,
And living by the Norm that they expound
And teach. Hence are recluses dear to me. (279)

Learn'd and proficient in the Norm; elect,
And living by the Doctrine; self-possessed,
Intent. Hence are recluses dear to me. (280)

Far and remote they wander, self-possessed,
Wise in their words and meek, they know the end
Of ill. Hence are recluses dear to me. (281)

And when along the village street they go,
At naught they turn to look; incurious
They walk. Hence are recluses dear to me. (282)

They lay not up a treasure for the flesh,
Nor storehouse-jar nor crate. The Perfected
Their Quest. Hence are recluses dear to me. (283)

They clutch no coin; no gold their hand doth take,
Nor silver. For their needs sufficient yields
The day. Hence are recluses dear to me. (284)

From many a clan and many a countryside
They join the Order, mutually bound
In love. Hence are recluses dear to me.' (285)

'Now truly for our weal, O Rohiṇī,
Wert thou a daughter born into this house !
Thy trust is in the Buddha and the Norm
And in the Order; keen thy piety. (286)
 For well thou know'st this is the Field supreme
Where merit may be wrought. We too henceforth
Will minister ourselves to holy men.
For thereby shall accrue to our account
A record of oblations bounteous.' (287)

'If Ill thou fearest, if thou like it not,
Go thou and seek the Buddha and the Norm,
And Order for thy refuge; learn of them
And keep the Precepts. So shalt thou find weal.' (288)

'Lo ! to the Buddha, I for refuge go
And to the Norm and Order. I will learn
Of them to take upon myself and keep
The Precepts. So shall I indeed find weal. (289)

Once but a son of brahmins born was I.
To-day I stand brahmin in very deed.
The nobler Threefold Wisdom have I won,

Won the true Veda-lore, and graduate
Am I from better Sacrament returned,
Cleansed by the inward spiritual bath. (290)

For the brahmin, established in the Refuges and the
Precepts, when later on he became alarmed, renounced the world,
and developing insight, was established in Arahantship. Reflecting
on his attainment, he exulted in that last verse.

LXVIII

Cāpā.

She, too, having made her resolve under former Buddhas,
and heaping up good of age-enduring efficacy in this and that
rebirth, till she had accumulated the sources of good, and matured
the conditions for emancipation, was, in this Buddha-age, reborn
in the Vaṅkahāra country, at a certain village of trappers, as the
daughter of the chief trapper, and named Cāpa. And at that time
Upaka, an ascetic, met the Master as he was going to Benares,
there to set rolling from his Bo-tree throne the Wheel of the
Norm, and asked him: 'You seem, my friend, in perfect health !
Clear and pure is your complexion. Wherefore have you, friend,
left the world ? or who may your teacher be ? or whose doctrine do
you believe in ?' And he was thus answered:

'All have I overcome. All things I know,
'Mid all things undefiled. Renouncing all,
In death of Craving wholly free. My own
The Deeper View. Whom should I name to thee ?
For me no teacher lives. I stand alone
On earth, 'mong devas rival to me there's none.

Now go I on seeking Benares town,
To start the Wheel, the gospel of the Norm,

To rouse and guide the nations blind and lost,
Striking Salvation's drum, Ambrosia's alarm.'

The ascetic, discerning the omniscience and great mission of
the Master, was comforted in mind, and replied: 'Friend, may
these things be ! Thou art worthy to be a conqueror, world
without end !' Then, taking a by-road, he came to the Vaṅkahāra
country, and abode near the hamlet of the trappers, where the head
trapper supplied his wants. One day the latter, setting off on a
long hunt with sons and brothers, bade his daughter not neglect
'the Arahant' in his absence. Now, she was of great beauty; and
Upaka, seeking alms at her home, and captivated by her beauty,
could not eat, but took his food home, and laid down fasting,
vowing he would die should he not win Cāpā. After seven days the
father returned, and, on inquiring for his 'Arahant', heard he had
not come again after the first day. The trapper sought him, and
Upaka, moaning, and rolling over, confessed his plight. The
trapper asked if he knew any craft, and he answered, 'No'; but
offered to fetch their game and sell it. The trapper consented, and,
giving him a coat, brought him to his own home, and gave him his
daughter. In due time she had a son, whom they called Subhadda.
Cāpā, when the baby cried, sang to him: 'Upaka's boy, ascetic's
boy, game-dealer's boy, don't cry, don't cry !' mocking her
husband. And he said at length: 'Do not thou, Cāpā, fancy I have
none to protect me. I have a friend, even a conqueror eternal, and
to him I will go.' She saw that he was vexed, and teased him again
and again in the same way, till one day, in anger, he got ready to
go. She said much, but vainly, to prevent him, and he set out
westward. And the Exalted One was then at Sāvatthī in the Jeta
Grove, and announced this to the brethren: 'He who to-day shall
come asking, "Where is the Conqueror eternal ?" send him to me.'
And Upaka arrived, and, standing in the midst of the Vihāra,
asked: 'Where is the Conqueror eternal ?' So they brought him,
and when he saw the Exalted One, he said: 'Dost know me,
Exalted One ?' 'Yea, I know. But thou, where hast thou spent the
time ?' 'In the Vaṅkahāra country, lord.' 'Upaka, thou art now an
old man; canst thou bear the religious life ?' 'I will enter thereon,

lord.' The Master bade a certain Bhikkhu, 'Come, do thou, Bhikkhu, ordain him.' And he thereafter exercising and training himself, was soon established in the Fruition of the Path-of-No-Return, and thereupon died, being reborn in the Aviha heavens. At the moment of that rebirth he attained Arahantship.

Seven have thus attained it, as it has been said.

But Cāpā, sick at heart over his departure, delivered her boy to his grandfather, and, following the way Upaka had gone, renounced the world at Sāvatthī, and attained Arahantship. And uniting Upaka's verses with her own, she thus exulted:

(*Her husband speaks*)

'Once staff in hand homeless I fared and free.
Now but a trapper am I, sunken fast
In baneful bog of earthly lusts, yet fain
To come out on the yonder side. My wife (291)
Plays with her child and mocks my former state,
Deeming her charm yet holdeth me in thrall.
But I will cut the knot and roam again. (292)

Cāpā

'O be not angry with me, hero mine !
O thou great prophet, be not wroth with me !
For how may he who giveth place to wrath
Attain to holy life and purity ? (293)

Husband

'Nay, I'll go forth from Nāla. Who would live
At Nāla now, where he who fain to lead
A life of righteousness sees holy men

Beguiled by the beauty of a girl !' (294)

Cāpā

'O turn again, my dark-eyed lover, come
And take thy fill of Cāpā's love for thee,
And I, thy slave, will meet thy every wish,
And all my kinsfolk shall thy servants be.' (295)

Husband

'Nay, were a man desirous of thy love,
He well might glory didst thou promise him
A fourth of what thou temp'st me here withal !' (296)

Cāpā

'O dark-eyed love, am I not fair to see,
As the liana swaying in the woods,
As the pomegranate-tree in fullest bloom
Growing on hill-top, or the trumpet-flower
Drooping o'er mouth of island cavern ? See, (297)
With crimson sandal-wood perfumed, I'll wear
Finest Benares robe for thee — O why,
O how wilt thou go far away from me ?' (298)

Husband

'Ay ! so the fowler seeketh to decoy
His bird. Parade thy charms e'en as thou wilt,
Ne'er shalt thou bind me to thee as of yore.' (299)

Cāpā

'And this child-blossom, O my husband, see
Thy gift to me — now surely thou wilt not
Forsake her who hath borne a child to thee ?' (300)

Husband

'Wise men forsake their children, wealth and kin,
Great heroes ever go forth from the world,
As elephants sever their bonds in twain.' (301)

Cāpā

'Then this thy child straightway with stick or axe
I'll batter on the ground — to save thyself
From mourning for thy son thou wilt not go !' (302)

Husband

'And if thou throw the child to jackels, wolves,
Or dogs, child-maker without ruth, e'en so
'Twill not avail to turn me back again !' (303)

Cāpā

'Why, then, go if thou must, and fare thee well.
But tell me to what village wilt thou go,
What town or burg or city is thy goal ?' (304)

Husband

'In the past days we went in fellowship,
Deeming our shallow practice genuine.
Pilgrims we wandered — hamlet, city, town,
And capital — we tramped to each in turn.' (305)
'But the Exalted Buddha now doth preach,
Along the banks of the Nerañjarā,
The Norm whereby all may be saved from ill.
To him I go; he now my guide shall be.' (306)

Cāpā

'Yea, go, and take my homage unto him
Who is the supreme Sovran of the World,
And making salutation by the right,
Do thou from us to him make offering.' (307)

Husband

'Now meet and right is this, e'en as thou say'st,
That I in doing homage, speak for thee
To him, the Supreme Sovran of the World.
And making salutation by the right,
I'll render offering for thee and me.' (308)

So Kāḷa went to the Nerañjarā,
And saw the very Buddha on the bank,
Teaching the Way Ambrosial: of Ill, (309)
And of how Ill doth rise, and how Ill may
Be overpast, and of the way thereto,

Even the Ariyan, the Eightfold Path. (310)
Low at his feet the husband homage paid,
Saluted by the right and Cāpā's vows
Presented; then the world again renounced
For homeless life; the Threefold Wisdom won,
And brought to pass the bidding of the Lord. (311)

LXIX

Sundarī.

She too, having made her resolve under former Buddhas, and
heaping up good of age-enduring efficacy in this and that rebirth,
was reborn thirty-one aeons ago, when Vessabhu was Buddha, in a
clansman's family. One day she ministered to the Master with
alms, and worshipped him, and he perceived her believing heart,
and thanked her. After celestial and other happy rebirths, her
knowledge having come to maturity, she was, in this Buddha-age,
reborn at Benares as the daughter of Sujāta, a brahmin. Because of
her perfect form they called her Sundarī (Beauty). When she grew
up, her younger brother died. Her father, overmastered by grief,
and going to and fro, met the Therī Vāsiṭṭhī. When she asked him
what afflicted him, he answered as in the first two verses.
Wishing to allay his grief, she spoke the next two verses, and told
him of her own griefless state. The brahmin asked her: 'How,
lady, did you become free from grief (*a-sokā*)?' The Therī told him
of the Three Jewels, the Refuges. 'Where,' he asked, 'is the
Master?' 'He is now at Mithilā.' So the brahmin drove in his
carriage to Mithilā and sought audience of the Master. To him the
Master taught the Norm; and he believed, and entered the Order,
attaining Arahantship on the third day, after strenuous effort in
establishing insight.

But the charioteer drove his chariot back to Benares, and
told the brahmin-woman what had taken place. When Sundarī
heard of it, she asked her mother, saying: 'Mother, I too would

leave the world.' The mother said: 'All the wealth in this house belongs to you. You are the heiress of this family. Take up your heritage and enjoy it. Go not forth.' But Sundarī said: 'Wealth is no use to me. Mother, I would leave the world;' and, bringing the mother to consent, she abandoned her great possessions like so much spittle, and entered the Order (at Benares). And studying and striving because of the promise in her and the maturity of her knowledge, she attained Àrahantship, with thorough grasp of the Norm in form and meaning.

Dwelling thereafter in the ease of fruition and the bliss of Nibbāna, she thought: 'I will utter a Lion's Roar before the Master.' And asking permission of her teacher, she left Benares, accompanied by a great following of Bhikkhunīs, and in due course came to Sāvatthī, did obeisance to the Master, and stood on one side. Welcomed by him, she declared her (attainment of) wisdom by extolling her relation to him as the 'daughter of his mouth,' and so on. Thereupon all her kinsfolk, beginning with her mother, and their attendants, renounced the world. She, reflecting on her attainment, and using her father's utterances in her own Psalm, exulted as follows:

Sujāta

Dame of the brahmins, thou too in the past —
Thou knowest — 'twas thy little babes Death robbed
And preyed upon; and thou all night, all day
Madest thy bitter wail. Vāsiṭṭhī, say ! (312)
How comes it that to-day thou, who hast lost
So many — was it seven ? — all thy sons,
No more dost mourn and weep so bitterly ? (313)

Vāsiṭṭhī

Nay, brahmin, many hundreds of our babes,
And of our kinsfolk many hundred more,
Have we in all the ages past and gone
Seen preyed upon by Death, both you and I. (314)
But I have learnt how from both Birth and Death
A way there is t' escape. Wherefore no more
I mourn, no weep, nor make my bitter wail. (315)

Sujāta

Wondrous in sooth, Vāsiṭṭhī, are the words
Thou speakest ! Whose the doctrine thou hast learnt ?
Whence thine authority for speech like this ? (316)

Vāsiṭṭhī

'Tis He, the Very Wake, the Buddha, He
Who late, hard by the town of Mithilā,
Did teach the Norm, brahmin, whereby
All that hath life may put off every ill. (317)
When I, O brahmin, when I heard the Arahant
Reveal the Doctrine of the Non-Substrate,
Forthwith the Gospel sank into my heart,
And all my mother-grief fell off from me. (318)

Sujāta

Then I too straight will go to Mithilā,
If haply the Exalted Buddha may
Me, even me, release from every ill. (319)

The brahmin went; he saw the Awaken'd One,
Th' Emancipated, Him in whom
No base is found for rebirth, and from Him,
The Seer, Him who hath passed beyond all ill, (320)
He heard the Norm: the Truth of Ill, and how
Ill comes, and how Ill may be overpassed,
E'en by the Ariyan, the Eightfold Path,
That leadeth to the abating of all Ill. (321)
Forthwith the Gospel sank into his heart.
He left the world, he chose the homeless life.
On the third night of contemplation rapt,
Sujāta touched and won the Threefold Lore. (322)

Sujāta

Come charioteer, now drive this chariot home !
Wish thy good mistress health, the brahmin-woman,
And say: 'The brahmin hath renounced the world.
On the third night of contemplation rapt
Sujāta touched and won the Threefold Lore.' (323)

And so the driver took the car and purse
Of money home, and wished his mistress health,
And said: 'The brahmin hath renounced the world.
On the third night of contemplation rapt

Sujāta touched and won the Threefold Lore.' (324)

Sundarī's Mother

For this that thou hast heard, O Charioteer,
And tellest: that the brahmin hath attained
The Threefold Lore, no half-gift give I thee.
Take thou the chariot, take the horses both,
And take a thousand pieces for thy pains. (325)

Charioteer

Let them remain thine own, O brahmin-woman,
Horses and chariot and the thousand coins,
For I, too, have a mind to leave the world,
Near him of chiefest wisdom to abide. (326)

Sundarī's Mother

But thou, my Sundarī, now that thy father hath gone forth,
Leaving his home, renouncing all his great estate,
Cattle and horses, elephants, jewels and rings,
Thou dost at least come to thine own ! Thou art the heir
Of this thy family. Do thou enjoy thy wealth. (327)

Sundarī

Cattle and horses, elephants, jewels and rings —
Ay, all that goes to make this fair and broad estate
Hath he put far from him, my father dear,
And left the world, afflicted for his son.

I, too, afflicted at my brother's death,
I have a mind like him to leave the world. (328)

Sundarī's Mother

May this, then, thine intention, Sundarī,
Thy heart's desire, be crowned with success !
The food from hand to mouth, glean'd here and there,
The patchwork robe — these things accomplished
Will purify in other after-world
Whate'er has poisoned life for thee in this. (329)

Sundarī

I've trained me, Lady, in the threefold course.
Clear shines for me the Eye Celestial.
I know the how and when I came to be
Down the long past, and where it was I lived. (330)
To thee I owe it, O thou noble friend,
Thou loveliest of the Therī Sisterhood,
That I the Threefold Lore have gotten now,
And that the Buddha's will hath been obeyed. (331)
Give to me, Lady, thy consent, for I
Would go to Sāvatthī, so that I may
Utter my 'lion's roar', — my 'Hail, all hail !' —
In presence of the Buddha, Lord and Chief. (332)

See, Sundarī, the Master fair in hue,
His countenance as fine gold, clear and bright,
Him who is All-enlightened, Buddha, Best,
Tamer of untamed, never tasting fear. (333)

And see, O Master, Sundarī, who comes
To tell thee of Emancipation won,
And of the right no more to be reborn.
Who hath herself from passion freed,
Unyoked from bondage, loosened from the world.
Accomplished now is her appointed work,
And all that drugged her heart is purged away. (334)

Sundarī

Lo ! from Benares I am come to thee —
I, Sundarī, thy pupil, at thy feet,
O mighty Hero, see me worship here. (335)
Thou art Buddha ! thou art Master ! and thine,
Thy daughter am I, issue of thy mouth,
Thou Very Brahmin ! even of thy word
Accomplished now is my appointed task,
And all that drugged my heart is purged away. (336)

Buddha

Welcome to thee, thou gracious maiden ! thence
For thee 'twas but a little way to come.
For so they come who, victors over self,
Are fain to worship at the Master's feet,
Who also have themselves from passion freed,
Unyoked from bondage, loosened from the world,
Who have accomplished their appointed task,
And all that drugged their hearts have purged away. (337)

LXX

Subhā.
(*The Goldsmith's Daughter*)

She, too, having made her resolve under former Buddhas, and heaping up good of age-enduring efficacy, so that she had progressively planted the root of good and accumulated the conditions of emancipation, was, in this Buddha-era, reborn at Rājagaha as the daughter of a certain goldsmith. From the beauty of her person she was called Subhā. Come to years of discretion, she went one day, while the Master was at Rājagaha, and belief in him had come to her, and did obeisance, seating herself on one side. The Master, seeing the maturity of her moral faculties, and in accordance with her wish, taught her the Norm enshrined in the Four Truths. She was thereby established in the fruition of Stream-entry, which is in countless ways adorned. Later she realized the disadvantages of domestic life, and entered the Order under the Great Pajāpatī the Gotamid, devoting herself to the higher Paths. From time to time her relations invited her to return to the world, urging its charms. To them thus come one day, she set forth the danger in house-life and in the world, preaching the Norm in the twenty-four verses below, and dismissed them cured of their desire. She then strove for insight, purifying her faculties, till at length she won Arahantship. As Arahant she spoke thus:

A maiden I, all clad in white, once heard
The Norm, and hearkened eager, earnestly,
So in me rose discernment of the Truths. (338)
Thereat all worldly pleasures irked me sore,
For I could see the perils that beset
This reborn compound, 'personality',
And to renounce it was my sole desire. (339)

So I forsook my world — my kinsfolk all,
My slaves, my hirelings, and my villages,
And the rich fields and meadows spread around,
Things fair and making for the joy of life —
All these I left, and sought the Sisterhood,
Turning my back upon no mean estate. (340)

Amiss were't now that I, who in full faith
Renounced that world, who well discerned the Truth,
Who, laying down what gold and silver bring,
Cherish no worldly wishes whatsoe'er,
Should, all undoing, come to you again ! (341)
Silver and gold avail not to awake,
Or soothe. Unmeet for consecrated lives,
They are not Ariyan — not noble — wealth. (342)
Whereby greed is aroused and wantonness,
Infatuation and all fleshly lusts,
Whence cometh fear for loss and many a care:
Here is no ground for lasting steadfastness. (343)
Here men, heedless and maddened with desires,
Corrupt in mind, by one another let
And hindered, strive in general enmity. (344)
Death, bonds, and torture, ruin, grief, and woe
Await the slaves of sense, and dreadful doom. (345)
Why herewithal, my kinsmen — nay, my foes —
Why yoke me in your minds with sense-desires ?
Know me as one who saw, and therefore fled,
The perils rising from the life of sense. (346)
Not gold nor money can avail to purge
The poison of the deadly Āsavas.
Ruthless and murderous are sense-desires;

Foemen of cruel spear and prison-bonds. (347)
Why herewithal, my kinsmen — nay, my foes —
Why yoke me in your minds with sense-desires ?
Know me as her who fled the life of sense,
Shorn of her hair, wrapt in her yellow robe. (348)
The food from hand to mouth, glean'd here and there,
The patchwork robe — these things are meet for me,
The base and groundwork of the homeless life. (349)

Great sages spue forth all desires of sense,
Whether they be in heaven or on earth;
At peace they dwell, for they freeholders are,
For they have won unfluctuating bliss. (350)
Ne'er let me follow after worldly lusts,
Wherein no refuge is; for they are foes,
And murderers, and cruel blazing fires. (351)
Oh ! but an incubus is here, the haunt
Of dread and fear of death, a thorny brake,
A greedy maw it is, a path impassable,
Mouth of a pit wherein we lose our wits, (352)
A horrid shape of doom impending — such
Are worldly lusts; uplifted heads of snakes.
Therein they that be fools find their delight —
The blinded, general, average, sensual man. (353)

For all the many souls, who thus befooled
Err ignorant in the marsh of worldly lusts,
Heed not that which can limit birth and death. (354)

Because of worldly lusts mankind is drawn
By woeful way to many a direful doom —

Where ev'ry step doth work its penalty. (355)

Breeders of enmity are worldly lusts,
Engendering remorse and vicious taints.
Flesh baits, to bind us to the world and death. (356)

Leading to madness, to hysteria,
To ferment of the mind, are worldly lusts,
Fell traps by Māra laid to ruin men. (357)

Endless the direful fruit of worldly lusts,
Surcharged with poison, sowing many ills,
Scanty and brief its sweetness, stirring strife,
And withering the brightness of our days. (358)

For me who thus have chosen, ne'er will I
Into the world's disasters come again,
For in Nibbāna is my joy alway. (359)

So, fighting a [good] fight with worldly lusts,
I wait in hope for the Cool Blessedness,
Abiding earnest in endeavour, till
Nought doth survive that fetters me to them. (360)

This is my way, the Way that leads past grief,
Past all that doth defile, the haven sure,
Even the Ariyan Eightfold Path, called Straight.
There do I follow where the Saints have crossed. (361)

See now this Subhā, standing on the Norm,
Child of a craftsman in the art of gold !

Behold ! she hath attained to utter calm;
Museth in rapture 'neath the spreading boughs. (362)
To-day, the eighth it is since she went forth
In faith, and radiant in the Gospel's light.
By Uppalavaṇṇā instructed, lo !
Thrice wise is she and conqueror over death. (363)

Freed woman she, discharged is all her debt,
A Bhikkhunī, trained in the higher sense,
All sundered are the Bonds, her task is done,
And the great Drugs that poisoned her are purged. (364)

To her came Sakka, and his band of gods
In all their glory, worshipping Subhā,
Child of a craftsman in the art of gold,
But lord of all things that have life and breath. (365)

When, on the eighth day after her ordination, she won
Arahantship, attaining fruition, seated beneath a tree, the Exalted
One uttered these three verses (362-364) in her praises, pointing
her out to the Brethren. And the last verse was added by them who
recited (the canon at the Council), to celebrate Sakka's adoration.

CANTO XIV

PSALM OF ABOUT THIRTY VERSES

LXXI

Subhā of Jīvaka's Mango-grove.

She too, having made her resolve under former Buddhas, and heaping up good of age-enduring efficacy in this and that rebirth, fostering the root of good and perfecting the conditions for emancipation through the ripening of her knowledge, was in this Buddha-era reborn at Rājagaha, in the family of a very eminent brahmin. Her name was Subhā, and truly lovely was her body in all its members. It was for this reason that she came to be so called. While the Master sojourned at Rājagaha, she received faith and became a lay-disciple. Later she grew anxious over the round of life, and saw the bane of the pleasures of sense, and discerned that safety lay in renunciation. She entered the Order under the Great Pajāpatī the Gotamid, and exercising herself in insight, was soon established in the fruition of the Path of No-return.

Now one day a certain libertine of Rājagaha, in the prime of youth, was standing in the Jīvaka Mango-grove, and saw her going to siesta; and feeling enamoured, he barred her way, soliciting her to sensual pleasures. She declared to him by many instances the bane of sensuous pleasures and her own choice of renunciation, teaching him the Norm. Even then he was not cured, but persisted. The Therī, not stopping short at her own words, and seeing his passion for the beauty of her eyes, extracted one of them, and handed it to him, saying: 'Come, then ! here is the offending eye of her !' Thereat the man was horrified and appalled and, his lust all gone, asked her forgiveness. The Therī went to the Master's presence, and there, at sight of Him, her eye became as it was before. Thereat she stood vibrating with unceasing joy at the Buddha. The Master, knowing the state of her mind, taught her, and showed her exercise for reaching the highest. Repressing

her joy, she developed insight, and attained Arahantship, together
with thorough grasp of the Norm in form and meaning.
Thereafter, abiding in the bliss and fruition of Nibbāna, she,
reflecting on what she had won, uttered her dialogue with the
libertine in these verses:

In Jīvaka's pleasant woodland walked Subhā
The Bhikkhunī. A gallant met her there
And barred the way. To him thus spake Subhā. (366)

'What have I done to offend thee, that thus in my path thou
comest ?
No man, O friend, it beseemeth to touch a Sister in Orders.
(367)

So hath my Master ordained in the precepts we honour and
follow;
So hath the Welcome One taught in the training wherein
they have trained me,
Purified discipline holy. Why standest thou blocking my
pathway ? (368)
Me pure, thou impure of heart; me passionless, thou of vile
passions;
Me who as to the whole of me freed am in spirit and
blameless,
Me whence comes it that Thou dost hinder, standing
obnoxious ?' (369)

'Young art thou, maiden, and faultless — what seekest thou
in the holy life?
Cast off that yellow-hued raiment and come ! in the
blossoming woodland

Seek we our pleasure. Filled with the incense of blossoms the trees waft (370)
Sweetness. See, the spring's at the prime, the season of happiness !
Come with me then to the flowering woodland, and seek we our pleasure. (371)
Sweet overhead is the sough of the blossoming crests of the forest
Swayed by the Wind-gods. But an thou goest alone in the jungle,
Lost in its depths, how wilt thou find aught to delight or content thee ? (372)
Haunted is the great forest with many a herd of wild creatures,
Broken its peace by the tramplings of elephants rutting and savage.
Empty of mankind and fearsome — is't there thou would'st go uncompanioned ? (373)

Thou like a gold-wrought statue, like nymph in celestial garden
Movest, O peerless creature. Radiant would shine thy loveliness
Robed in raiment of beauty, diaphanous gear of Benares. (374)
I would live but to serve thee, an thou would'st abide in the woodland.
Dearer and sweeter to me than art thou in the world is no creature,
Thou with the languid and slow-moving eyes of an elf of the forest. (375)

If thou wilt list to me, come where the joys of the sheltered life wait thee;
Dwell in a house of verandas and terraces, handmaidens serving thee. (376)
Robe thyself in delicate gear of Benares, don garlands, use unguents.
Ornaments many and divers I give to thee, fashioned with precious stones,
Gold work and pearls. And thou shalt mount on a couch fair and sumptuous, (377)
Carved in sandalwood, fragrant with essences, spread with new pillows,
Coverlets fleecy and soft, and decked with immaculate canopies. (378)
Like to a lotus upborne on the bosom of sprite-haunted water.
Thou, O chaste anchorite, farest to old age, thy beauty unmated.' (379)

'What now to thee, in this carrion-filled, grave-filling carcase so fragile
Seen by thee, seemeth to warrant the doctrine thou speakest, infatuate ?' (380)

'Eyes hast thou like the gazelle's, like an elf's in the heart of the mountains;
'Tis those eyes of thee, sight of which feedeth the depth of my passion. (381)
Shrined in thy dazzling, immaculate face as in calyx of lotus,
'Tis those eyes of thee, sight of which feedeth the strength of my passion. (382)

Though thou be far from me, how could I ever forget thee, O maiden,

Thee of the long-drawn eyelashes, thee of the eyes so miraculous ?

Dearer to me than those orbs is naught, O thou witching-eyed fairy !' (383)

'Lo ! thou art wanting to walk where no path is; thou seekest to capture

Moon from the skies for thy play; thou would'st jump o'er the ridges of Meru,

Thou who presumest to lie in wait for a child of the Buddha ! (384)

Nowhere in earth or in heaven lives now any object of lust for me.

Him I know not. What like is he ? Slain, root and branch, through the Noble Path. (385)

Hurled as live coal from the hand, and rated as deadly as poison-cup,

Him I see not. What like is he ? Slain, root and branch, through the Noble Path. (386)

Tempt thou some woman who hath not discerned what I say, or whose teacher

Is but a learner; haply she'll listen; tempt thou not Subhā;

She understandeth. And now 'tis thyself hast vexation and failure. (387)

For I have set my mind to be watchful in whatso befalls me —

Blame or honour, gladness or sorrow, and knowing the principle:—

'Foul are all composite things,' nowhere the mind of me
clings to them. (388)

Yea, the disciple am I of the Welcome One; onward the
march of me
Riding the Car of the Road that is Eightfold. Drawn are the
arrows
Out of my wounds, and purged is my spirit of drugging
Intoxicants.
So I am come to haunts that are Empty.   There lies my
pleasure. (389)

Oh ! I have seen it — a puppet well painted, with new
wooden spindles,
Cunningly fastened with strings and with pins, and diversely
dancing. (390)
But if the strings and the pins be all drawn out and loosened
and scattered,
So that the puppet be made non-existent and broken in
pieces,
Which of the parts wilt thou choose and appoint for thy
heart's rest and solace ? (391)
Such is the manner wherein persist these poor little bodies:
Take away members and attributes — nothing surviveth in
any wise.
Nothing surviveth!   Which dost thou choose for thy
heart's rest and solace ? (392)
E'en as a fresco one sees drawn on a wall, painted in ochre,
[Giveth us naught of the true and the real, save in the
seeming;]
Thou herein with vision perverted [canst not distinguish;

Judgest with] wisdom of average human, fallible, worthless. (393)
O thou art blind ! thou chasest a sham, deluded by puppet shows
Seen in the midst of the crowd; thou deemest of value and genuine
Conjurer's trickwork, trees all of gold that we see in our dreaming. (394)
What is this eye but a little ball lodged in the fork of a hollow tree,
Bubble of film, anointed with tear-brine, exuding slime-drops,
Compost wrought in the shape of an eye of manifold aspects ?' (395)

Forthwith the maiden so lovely tore out her eye and gave it him:
Here, then ! take thou thine eye !' Nor sinned she, her heart unobstructed. (396)
Straightway the lust in him ceased and he her pardon imploring:
'O that thou mightest recover thy sight, thou maid pure and holy !
Never again will I dare to offend thee after this fashion. (397)
Sore hast thou smitten my sin; blazing flames have I clasped to my bosom;
Poisonous snake have I handled — but O ! be thou heal'd and forgive me !' (398)
Freed from molesting, the Bhikkhunī went on her way to the Buddha,

Chief of th' Awakened. There in his presence, seeing those
features
Born of uttermost merit, straightway her sight was restored
to her. (399)

CANTO XV

PSALM OF OVER FORTY VERSES

LXXII

Isidāsī.

She too, having made her resolve under former Buddhas, and persisting in her former disposition in this and that rebirth, in that she heaped up good of age-enduring efficacy, in the seventh rebirth before her last phase of life, susceptible to sex-attraction, wrought adulterous conduct. For this she did purgatory for many centuries, and thereafter for three rebirths was an animal. Thereafter she was brought forth by a slave-woman as an hermaphrodite, and thereafter she was born as the daughter of a poor common man, and was, when of age, married to the son of a caravan-leader named Giridāsa. Now the wife that he had was virtuous and of noble qualities, and the new wife envied her, and quarrelled with the husband because of her. After her death she was, in this Buddha-era, reborn at Ujjenī as the daughter of a virtuous, honoured and wealthy merchant, and was named Isidāsī. When she was of age, her parents gave her in marriage to a merchant's son, a good match with herself. For a month she dwelt with him as a devoted wife; then, as the fruit of her previous actions, her husband became estranged from her, and turned her out of his house. All this is told in the Pali text. Because she had not proved desirable for one husband after another, she grew agitated and, gaining her father's consent, took orders under the Therī Jinadattā. And studying for insight, she not long after attained Arahantship, together with thorough grasp of the Norm in form and meaning.

Dwelling in the bliss of fruition and Nibbāna, she one day, after seeking her meal in the city of Patna and dining, sat down on a sandbank of great Ganges, and being asked by her companion, the Therī Bodhi, about her previous experience, she related it by

way of verses. And to show the connection of her former and
latter replies, these three stanzas were inserted by the
Recensionists:

In the fair city of Patna, earth's fairest city,
Named for its beauty after the Trumpet-flower,
Dwelt two saintly Sisters, born of the Sākiyas, (400)
Isidāsī the one, Bodhi the other.
Precept-observers, lovers of Jhāna-rapture,
Learned ladies and cleansed from the taint of all worldliness.
(401)
These having made their round, and broken their fasting,
Washed their bowls, and sitting in happy seclusion,
Spake thus one to the other, asking and answering: (402)

'Thou hast a lovely mien, Isidāsī,
Fresh and unwithered yet thy woman's prime,
What flaw in the life yonder hast thou seen,
That thou didst choose surrender for thy lot ?' (403)
Then in that quiet spot Isidāsī,
Skilled in the exposition of the Norm,
Took up her tale and thus did make reply:
'Hear, Bodhi, how it was that I came forth. (404)

In Ujjenī, Avantī's foremost town,
My father dwells, a virtuous citizen,
His only daughter I, his well-beloved,
The fondly cherished treasure of his life. (405)
Now from Sāketa came a citizen
Of the first rank and rich exceedingly
To ask my hand in marriage for his son.
And father gave me him, as daughter-in-law. (406)

My salutation morn and eve I brought
To both the parents of my husband, low
Bowing my head and kneeling at their feet,
According to the training given me.   (407)
My husband's sisters and his brothers too,
And all his kin, scarce were they entered when
I rose in timid zeal and gave them place. (408)
And as to food, or boiled or dried, and drink,
That which was to be stored I set aside,
And served it out and gave to whom 'twas due. (409)
Rising betimes, I went about the house,
Then with my hands and feet well cleansed I went
To bring respectful greeting to my lord,   (410)
And taking comb and mirror, unguents, soap,
I dressed and groomed him as a handmaid might. (411)
I boiled the rice, *I* washed the pots and pans;
And as a mother on her only child,
So did I minister to my good man. (412)

For me, who with toil infinite thus worked,
And rendered service with a humble mind,
Rose early, ever diligent and good,
For me he nothing felt save sore dislike. (413)
Nay, to his mother and his father he
Thus spake:— 'Give ye me leave and I will go,
For not with Isidāsī will I live
Beneath one roof, nor ever dwell with her.' (414)

'O son, speak not on this wise of thy wife,
For wise is Isidāsī and discreet,
An early riser and a housewife diligent.

Say, doth she find no favour in thine eyes ?'   (415)

'In nothing doth she work me harm, and yet
With Isidāsī will I never live.
I cannot suffer her. Let be, let be !
Give ye me leave and I will go away.'   (416)
And when they heard, mother and father-in-law
Asked of me: 'What then hast thou done t' offend ?
Speak to us freely, child, and speak the truth.'   (417)

'Naught have I done that could offend, nor harm,
Nor nagged at evil words. What can I do,
That me my husband should so sore mislike ?'   (418)

To guard and keep their son, they took me back,
Unwilling guides, to father's house, distressed,
Distraught: 'Alas ! we're beaten, pretty Luck !'   (419)

Then father gave me for the second time as bride,
Content with half my husband's sire had paid.   (420)
From that house too, when I had dwelt a month,
I was sent back, though I had worked and served,
Blameless and virtuous, as any slave.   (421)
And yet a third, a friar begging alms —
One who had self controlled, and could control
Favour in fellow-men — my father met
And spake him thus: 'Be thou my son-in-law !
Come, throw away that ragged robe and pot !'   (422)
He came, and so we dwelt one half moon more
Together. Then to father thus he spake:
'O give me back my frock, my bowl and cup.

Let me away to seek once more my scraps.' (423)
Then to him father, mother, all the tribe
Of kinsfolk clamouring: 'What is it then
Here dwelling likes you not ? Say quick, what is't
That we can do to make you better pleased ?' (424)
Then he: 'If for myself I can suffice,
Enough for me. One thing I know:— beneath
One roof with Isidāsī I'll not live !' (425)

Dismissed he went. I too, alone I thought.
And then I asked my parents' leave to die,
Or, that they suffer me to leave the world. (426)
Now Lady Jinadattā on her beat
Came by my father's house for daily alms,
Mindful of every moral precept, she,
Learned and expert in the Vinaya. (427)

And seeing her we rose, and I prepared
A seat for her, and as she sat I knelt,
Then gave her food, both boiled and dried, (428)
And water — dishes we had set aside —
And satisfied her hunger. Then I said:
'Lady, I wish to leave the world.' 'Why here,' (429)
My father said, 'dear child, is scope for thee
To walk according to the Norm. With food
And drink canst gratify the holy folk
And the twice-born.' But of my father I, (430)
Weeping and holding out clasped hands, besought:
'Nay, but the evil karma I have done,
That would I expiate and wear away.' (431)
Then father said: 'Win thou Enlightenment

And highest Truth, and gain Nibbāna. That
Hath He, the Best of Beings, realized.' (432)

Then to my mother and my father dear,
And all my kinsfolk tribe I bade farewell.
And only seven days had I gone forth
Ere I had touched and won the Threefold Lore. (433)
Then did I come to know my former births,
E'en seven thereof, and how e'en now I reap
The harvest, the result, that then I sowed.
That will I now declare to thee, an thou
Wilt listen single-minded to my tale. (434)

In Erakaccha's town of yore I lived,
A wealthy craftsman in all works of gold.
Incensed by youth's hot blood, a wanton, I
Assailed the virtue of my neighbours' wives. (435)
Therefrom deceasing, long I cooked in hell,
Till, fully ripened, I emerged, and then
Found rebirth in the body of an ape. (436)
Scarce seven days I lived before the great
Dog-ape, the monkeys' chief, castrated me.
Such was the fruit of my lasciviousness. (437)
Therefrom deceasing in the woods of Sindh,
Reborn the offspring of a one-eyed goat (438)
And lame; twelve years a gelding, gnawn by worms,
Unfit, I carried children on my back.
Such was the fruit of my lasciviousness. (439)
Therefrom deceasing, I again found birth,
The offspring of a cattle-dealer's cow,
A calf of lac-red hue; in the twelfth month (440)

Castrated, yoked, I drew the plough and cart,
Purblind and worried, driven and unfit.
Such was the fruit of my lasciviousness. (441)
Therefrom deceasing, even in the street
I came to birth, child of a household slave,
Neither of woman nor of man my sex.
Such was the fruit of my lasciviousness. (442)
At thirty years of age I died, and was reborn
A girl, the daughter of a carter, poor
And of ill-fortune, and oppressed with debts
Incurred to usurers. To pay the sum   (443)
Of interest that ever grew and swelled,
In place of money, woeful little me
The merchant of a caravan dragged off,
Bearing me weeping from my home. (444)
Now in my sixteenth year, when I
Blossomed a maiden, that same merchant's son,
Giridāsa the name of him, loved me
And made me wife. Another wife he had, (445)
A virtuous dame of parts and of repute,
Enamoured of her mate. And thus I brought
Discord and enmity within that house. (446)

Fruit of my karma was it thus that they,
In this last life, have slighted me, e'en tho'
I waited on them as their humble slave.

Well ! of all that now have I made an end ! (447)

CANTO XVI

PSALM OF THE GREAT CHAPTER

LXXIII

Sumedhā.

She too, having made her resolve under former Buddhas, and heaping up good of age-enduring efficacy in this and that rebirth, thoroughly preparing the conditions of emancipation, was born, when Koṇāgamana was Buddha, in a clansman's family. When she was of age, she and her friends, clansmen's daughters, agreed together to have a great park made, and handed it over to the Buddha and his Order. Through the merit of that act, she was reborn in the heaven of the Three-and-Thirty. After a glorious period there, she arose once more among the Yāma gods, then among the Blissful gods, then among the Happy Creators, then among the Disposers of others' creations, and there became Queen of the King of the gods. Reborn thereafter, when Kassapa was Buddha, as the daughter of a wealthy citizen, she acquired splended merit as a lay-believer, winning another rebirth among the gods of the Three-and-Thirty. Finally reborn, in this Buddha-age, at the city of Mantāvatī, as the daughter of King Koñca, she was named Sumedhā. And when she was come to years of discretion, her mother and father agreed to let Anikaratta, the Rāja of Vāraṇavatī, see her. But she from her childhood had been in the habit of going with Princesses of her own age and attendant slaves to the Bhikkhunīs' quarters to hear them preach the Doctrine, and for a long time, because of her pristine resolve, she had grown fearful of birth in the round of life, devoted to religion and averse to the pleasures of sense.

Wherefore, when she heard the decision of her parents and kinsfolk, she said: 'My duty lies not in the life of the house. I will leave the world.' And they were not able to dissuade her. She thinking, 'Thus shall I gain permission to leave the world,' laid hold of her purpose, and cut off her own hair. Then using her hair in accordance with what she had heard from the Bhikkhunīs of their methods, she concentrated her attention of repugnance to physical attraction, and calling up the idea of 'Foul Things', then and there attained First Jhāna. And when she was thus rapt, her parents came to her apartments in order to give her away. But she made them first and all their retinue and all the Rāja's people believers in religion, and left the house, renouncing the world in the Bhikkhunīs' quarters.

Not long after, establishing insight, and ripe for emancipation, she attained Arahantship, with thorough grasp of the Norm in form and in meaning. And reflecting on her victory, she broke forth in exultation:

King Heron's daughter at Mantāvatī,
Born of his chief consort, was Sumedhā,
Devoted to the makers of the Law. (448)
A virtuous maid was she and eloquent,
Learned and in the system of our Lord
Well trained. She of her parents audience sought,
And spake: 'Now listen, mother, father, both ! (449)
All my heart's love is to Nibbāna given.
Transient is everything that doth become,
E'en if it have the nature of a god.
What truck have I, then, with the empty life
Of sense, that giveth little, slayeth much ? (450)
Bitter as serpents' poison are desires
Of sense, whereafter youthful fools do yearn.
For that full many a night in wretchedness
They drag out tortured lives in realms of woe. (451)
The vicious-minded, vicious doers mourn
In purgatorial lives. Ever are fools
Without restraint in deed and word and thought. (452)

Oh ! but the foolish have no wit or will.
They cannot grasp what maketh sorrow rise —
When taught, they learn not; in their slumb'ring minds
The Fourfold Ariyan Truth awakens not. (453)
Those Truths, O mother, that th' Awakened One,
The Best, the Buddha, hath revealed to us,
They, the Majority, know not, and they
Delight in coming aye again to be,
 And long to be reborn among the gods. (454)
E'en with the gods is no eternal home.
Becoming needs must be impermanent.
Yet they, the foolish souls, are not afraid
Again, again to come somewhere to birth. (455)
Four are the ways of doleful life, and two
Alone the ways of weal — and these how hard
To win ! Nor if one come into the four,
Is there renunciation from *that* world. (456)
Suffer ye both that I renounce my world;
And in the blessed teaching of the Lord,
Him of the Powers Ten, heedless of all
Without, I'll strive to root out birth and death. (457)
How can I take delight in many births,
In this poor body, froth without a soul ?
That I may put an utter end to thirst
Again to be, suffer that I go forth. (458)
Now is the Age of Buddhas ! Gone the want
Of oppportunity ! The moment's won !
O let me never while I live misprize
The precepts, nor withstand the holy life !' (459)

Thus spake Sumedhā, and again: 'Mother
And father mine, never again will I
As a laywoman break my fast and eat.
Here will I sooner lay me down and die !' (460)

Th' afflicted mother wept: the father, stunned
With grief, strove to dissuade and comfort her
Who prostrate lay upon the palace floor:— (461)
'Rise up, dear child. Why this unhappiness
For thee ? Thou art betrothed to go and reign
In Vāraṇavatī, the promised bride
Of King Anikaratta, handsome youth. (462)
Thou art to be his chief consort, his queen.
Hard is it, little child, to leave the world,
Hard are the precepts and the holy life. (463)
As queen thou wilt enjoy authority,
Riches and sov'reignty and luxuries.
Thou that art blest herein and young, enjoy
The sweets life yields. Let's to thy wedding, child.' (464)

Then answered them Sumedhā: 'Nay, not thus !
No soul, no essence, can becoming yield.
One or the other shall be — choose ye which:
Or let me leave the world, or let me die.
Thus, and thus only, would I choose to wed. (465)
What is it worth — this body foul, unclean,
Emitting odours, source of fears, a bag
Of skin with carrion filled, oozing impure (466)
The while ? What is it worth to me who know —
Repulsive carcass, plastered o'er with flesh
And blood, the haunt of worms, dinner of birds —

To whom shall such a thing as this be given ? (467)
Borne in a little while to charnel-field,
There is this body thrown, when mind hath sped,
Like useless log, from which e'en kinsfolk turn. (468)
Throwing the thing that they have bathed to be
The food of alien things, whereat recoil
The very parents, let alone their kin. (469)
They have a fondness for this soulless frame,
That's knit of bones and sinews, body foul,
Filled full of exudations manifold. (470)
Were one the body to dissect, and turn
The inside outermost, the smell would prove
Too much for e'en one's mother to endure. (471)
The factors of my being, organs, elements,
All are a transient compound, rooted deep
In birth, are Ill, and first and last the thing
I would not. Whom, then, could I choose to wed ? (472)
Rather would I find death day after day
With spears three hundred piercing me anew,
E'en for an hundred years, if this would then
Put a last end to pain, unending else. (473)
The wise would with this [bargain] close, and meet
Utter destruction, seeing that His Word,
The Master's runneth: "Long the wandering
Of them who, smitten, ever rise again." (474)
Countless the ways in which we meet our death,
'Mong gods and men, as demons or as beasts,
Among the shades, or in the haunts of hell. (475)
And there how many doomed tormented live !
No sure refuge is ours even in heaven.
Above, beyond Nibbāna's bliss, is naught. (476)

And they have won that Bliss who all their hearts
Have plighted to the blessed Word of Him
Who hath the Tenfold Power, and heeding naught,
Have striv'n to put far from them birth and death. (477)
This day, my father, will I get me forth !
I'll naught of empty riches! Sense-desires
Repel and sicken me, and are become
E'en as the stump where once hath stood a palm.' (478)

So spake she to her father. Now the King,
Anikaratta, on his way to woo
His youthful bride's consent, drew near
At the appointed time. But Sumedhā (479)
Let down the soft black masses of her hair
And with a dagger cut them off. Then closed
The door that led to her own terraced rooms,
And forthwith to First Jhāna-rapture won. (480)
There sat she lost in ecstasy, the while
Anikaratta reached the capital.
Then she fell musing on impermanence,
Developing the thought. Then is she ware (481)
The while Anikaratta swiftly mounts
The palace steps, in brave array of gems
And gold, and bowing low woos Sumedhā. (482)

'Reign in my kingdom and enjoy my wealth
And power. Rich, happy and so young thou art,
Enjoy the sweets that life and love can yield,
Though they be hard to win and won by few. (483)
To thee my kingdom I surrender ! Now
Dispose as thou dost wish; give gifts galore.

Be not downcast. Thy parents are distressed.' (484)

To him thus Sumedhā, for whom desires
Of sensuous love were worthless, nor availed
To lead astray, made answer: 'O set not
The heart's affections on this sensual love.
See all the peril, the satiety of sense. (485)
Mandhātā, King o' th' world's four continents,
Had greater wealth to gratify his sense
Than any other man, yet passed away
Unsatisfied, his wishes unfulfilled. (486)
Nay, an the rain-god rained all seven kinds
Of gems till earth and heaven were full, still would
The senses crave, and men insatiate die. (487)
"Like the sharp blades of swords are sense-desires."
"Like the poised heads of snakes prepared to dart."
"Like blazing torches", and "like bare gnawn bones." (488)
Transient, unstable are desires of sense,
Pregnant with Ill and full of venom dire,
Searing as heated iron globe to touch.
Baneful the root of them, baleful the fruit, (489)
As "fruit" that brings the climber to a fall,
Are sense-desires; evil as "lumps of flesh"
That greedy birds one from the other snatch;
As cheating "dreams"; as "borrowed goods" reclaimed.
(490)
"As spears and jav'lins are desires of sense,"
"A pestilence, a boil, and bane and bale.
A furnace of live coals", the root of bane,
Murderous and the source of harrowing dread. (491)

So hath the direfulness of sense-desires,
Those barriers to salvation, been declared.
Go, leave me, for I do not trust myself,
While in this world I yet have part and lot.   (492)
What shall another do for me ? For me
Whose head is wrapped in flames, whose steps are dogged
By age and death that tarry not. To crush
Them utterly I needs must strive.'   (493)

Then coming to her door she saw the king
Her suitor, and her parents seated there
And shedding tears. And once more spake to them: (494)

'Long have they yet to wander through the worlds
Who witless aye again their tears renew,
Weeping world without end for father dead,
Or brother slain, or that themselves must die.   (495)

Call ye to mind how it was said that tears
And milk and blood flow on world without end.
And bear in mind that tumulus of bones
By creatures piled who wander through the worlds.   (496)
Remember the four oceans as compared
With all the flow of tears and milk and blood.
Remember the "great cairn of one man's bones
From one aeon alone, equal to Vipula";   (497)
And how "great India would not suffice
To furnish little tally-balls of mould,
Wherewith to number all the ancestors
Of one's own round of life world without end."   (498)
Remember how "the little squares of straws

And boughs and twigs could ne'er suffice
As tallies for one's sires world without end." (499)
Remember how the parable was told
Of "purblind turtle in the Eastern Seas,
Or other oceans, once as time goes by,
Thrusting his head thro' hole of drifting yoke";
So rare as this the chance of human birth. (500)
Remember too the "body"-parable,
The "lump of froth", of spittle without core,
Drifting. See here the fleeting factors five.
And O forget not hell where many thole. (501)
Remember how we swell the charnel-fields,
Now dying, now again elsewhere reborn.
Remember what was said of "crocodiles",
And what those perils meant for us, and O !
Bear ye in mind the Four, the Ariyan Truths. (502)

The Nectar of the Norm is here ! O how
Canst thou be satisfied with bitter draughts
Of sense satiety ? All sensual joys
Are bitterer for the fivefold dogging Ill. (503)

The Nectar of the Norm is here ! O how
Canst thou be satisfied with fevered fits
Of sense-satiety ? All sensual joys
Are burning, boiling, ferment, stew. (504)

There is, where emnity is not ! O how
Canst thou be satisfied with joys of sense
Engend'ring thee so many foes — the wrath
Or greed of king, or thief, or rival, harm

Through fire, or water — yea, so many foes ! (505)

Emancipation waits ! O how canst thou
Be satisfied with sensual joys, wherein
Lie bonds and death ? Yea, in those very joys
Lurk gaol and headsman. They who seek t' indulge
Their lusts needs must thereafter suffer ills. (506)
Him will straw-torches burn who holds them long
And lets not go. So, in the parable,
Desires of sense burn them who let not go. (507)
Cast not away, because of some vain joy
Of sense, the vaster happiness sublime,
Lest like the finny carp thou gulp the hook,
Only to find thyself for that foredone. (508)
Tame thou thyself in sense-desires, nor let
Thyself be bound by them, as is a dog
Bound by a chain; else will they do forsooth
With thee as hungry pariahs with that dog. (509)
Once more I say, immeasurable Ills
And many weary miseries of mind
Thou'lt suffer yoked to sensual life. Renounce,
Renounce desires of sense ! They pass away. (510)

There is, that groweth never old ! O how
Canst thou be satisfied with sense-desires
That age so soon ? Are not all things reborn,
Where'er it be, gripped by disease and death? (511)
This that doth ne'er grow old, that dieth not,
This never-ageing, never-dying Path —
No sorrow cometh there, no enemies,
Nor is there any crowd, none faint or fail,

No fear cometh, nor aught that doth torment — (512)
To *this*, the Path Ambrosial, have gone
Full many. And to-day, e'en now 'tis to be won.
But only by a life that's utterly
Surrendered in devotion. Labour not,
And ye shall not attain !' Thus Sumedhā (513)
Ended her say, who found no joy in all
Activities that lead from life to life,
And, to Anikaratta thus her mind
Declaring, dropped her tresses on the floor. (514)
Then up he rose with outstretched folded hands,
And with her father pleaded for her thus:
'O suffer Sumedhā to leave the world,
That she may see the Truth and Liberty !' (515)

The parents suffered her, and forth she went,
Afeared to stay and build up fear and grief.
Six branches of Insight she realized,
As learner, winning to the Topmost Fruit. (516)

O wondrous this ! O marvellous in sooth !
Nibbāna for the daughter of a king !
Her state and conduct in her former births,
E'en as she told in her last life were these: (517)
'When Konāgamana was Buddha here,
And in a new abode, the Order's Park,
Took up his dwelling, two o' my friends, and I
Built a Vihāra for the Master's use. (518)
And many scores and centuries of lives
We lived among the gods, let alone men. (519)
Mighty our glory and our power among

The gods, nor need I speak of fame on earth.
Was I not consort of an Emperor,
The Treasure-Woman 'mongst the Treasures Seven ?
(520)

Endurance in the Truth the Master taught —
This was the cause, the source, the root,
This the First Link in the long Causal Line,
This is Nibbāna if we love the Norm.' (521)

Thus acting, they who put their trust in Him,
Wisdom Supreme, lose every wish and hope
Of coming back to be — and thus released
They from all passion's stain are purified. (522)

COMMENTATOR's ENVOI

The Psalms of them who through the Gospel's grace
Became the true-born children and the heirs,
Mouth-born, of Him who is the Master Blest,
King o' the Norm, creations of the Norm,
Excelling in all virtue, Arahants,
Who wrought all that 'twas possible to do —
These Psalms, their utterances when their wisdom
They did proclaim, or whensoe'er it was,
Beginning with Brother Subhūti's verse,
With Sisters' Psalms, headed by 'Sturdykin' —
All these the Leaders of the Order took,
And in one ordered serial compiled,
The *Theragāthā-Therīgāthā* named.

To elucidate the import of that work
Three Older Commentaries are extant.
Thereto this exegesis I have tried
T' indite, the which, in that where'er 'twas fit,
I strove to set the highest meaning forth,
I named the *Paramattha-Dīpanī*:
The whole whereof, now finished to the end,
By orderly decision is arranged,
For recitation from the sacred text,
In chapters of the number ninety-two.
Thus by the efficacy of such good
As has accrued to me, by me applied,
Have I made bright the glory of the word,
The system, of the Sovran of the world;
That, by their pure attainment in all truth
And virtue, mortals all may come to taste
The essence of emancipation won.
Long may the Very Buddha's Word and Law
Abide, and ever may it be revered
By every creature that hath life and breath !
And may the weather-god in season due
Send rain on earth, and may the powers that be
Govern the world as lovers of the Norm !

Thus endeth the Commentary on the Therīgāthā, by the Teacher, Brother Dhammapāla, residing at the Padara-Tittha-Vihāra.

APPENDIX

VERSES ATTRIBUTED TO SISTERS IN THE BHIKKHUNĪ-SAMYUTTA OF THE SAMYUTTA-NIKĀYA

1. Āḷavikā.

Thus have I heard. The Exalted One was once staying at Sāvatthī, in the Jeta Grove, the park of Anāthapiṇḍika. Now Āḷavikā the Bhikkhunī dressed herself early and, taking bowl and robe, entered Sāvatthī for food. And when she had gone about Sāvatthī for it, had broken her fast and returned, she entered the Dark Wood, seeking solitude.

Then Māra the Evil One, desiring to arouse fear, wavering, and dread in her, desiring to make her desist from being alone, went up to her, and addressed her in a verse:

'Ne'er shalt thou find escape while in the world.
What profiteth thee then thy loneliness ?
Take the good things of life while yet thou may'st,
Repentance else too late awaiteth thee.'

Then Āḷavikā thought: Who now is this, human or non-human, that speaketh this verse? Sure 'tis Māra the Evil One speaketh it, desirous to arouse in me fear, wavering and dread, desirous to make me desist from my solitude'. And Bhikkhunī Āḷavikā, knowing that 'twas he, replied with a verse:

'There is escape while in the world, and I
Have well attained thereto by insight won.
Thou evil limb of loafing ! 'tis not thine
To know that bourne, or how it may be reached.
Like spears and jav'lins are the joys of sense,
That pierce and rend the mortal frames of us.

These that thou callest "the good things of life,"
Good of that ilk to me is nothing worth.'

Then Māra, thinking, 'Bhikkhunī Ālavikā knows me !'
vanished thence, sad and dejected.

[In the following stories, the opening scene is the same as with
Ālavikā]

2. Somā.

Now Somā entered the Dark Wood for siesta, and, plunging
into its depths, sat down at the root of a certain tree for siesta.
The Māra the Evil One, desiring to arouse fear, wavering, and
dread in her, desiring to make her desist from concentrated
thought, went up to her, and addressed her in a verse:

'That vantage-ground the sages may attain is hard
To reach. With her two-finger consciousness
That is no woman competent to gain !'

Then Somā thought '[As Ālavikā] Sure 'tis Māra !' ... and
... replied with verses:

'What should the woman's nature do to them
Whose hearts are firmly set, who ever move
With growing knowledge onward in the Path ?
What can that signify to one in whom
Insight doth truly comprehend the Norm ?
To one for whom the question doth arise:
Am I a woman in these matters, or
Am I a man, or what not am I, then ?

To such a one are you, Sir, fit to talk !'

Then Māra, thinking, 'Bhikkhunī Somā knows me !' vanished thence, sad and dejected.

3. Gotamī.

Now the Lean Gotamid entered the Dark Wood for siesta, and, plunging into its depths, sat down at the root of a certain tree for siesta. Then Māra ... went up to her, and addressed her in a verse:

'How now ? Dost sit alone with tearful face
As mother stricken by the loss of child ?
Thou who hast plunged into the woods alone,
It is a man that thou hast come to seek ?'

Then the Lean Gotamid thought ... 'sure 'tis Māra !'... and replied with verses:

'Ay, ever am I she whose child is lost !
And for the seeking, there are men at hand.
I do not grieve, I am not shedding tears,
And so for thee, good sir, I fear thee not.
Slain everywhere is love of worldly joys,
And the thick gloom of ignorance is rent in twain.
Defeating all the army of the power of death.
I here abide purged of the poison-drugs.'

Then Māra, thinking, 'Bhikkhunī Gotamī knows me !' vanished thence, sad and dejected.

4. Vijayā.

Now Bhikkhunī Vijayā ... sat down at the root of a certain
tree for siesta. Then Māra ... addressed her in a verse:

'A maiden thou and beautiful — and I
So young a lad ! Now where to fivefold art
Of sounds melodious we may list, O come,
Lady, and let us take our fill of joy !'

The Bhikkhunī Vijayā thought ... 'Sure 'tis Māra !' ... and
replied with verses:

'Sights, sounds and tastes and smells and things to touch,
Wherein the mind delights, I leave them all
To thee, Māra; for such no mind have I !
This body vile, this brittle, crumbling thing,
Doth touch me only with distress and shame.
Craving for joys of sense is rooted out.
They who have come to worlds of form, and they
Who dwell where form is not, and that perfect
Attainment which is peace — from all,
From everywhere, the darkness is dispelled.'

Then Māra, thinking, 'Bhikkhunī Vijayā knows me !'
vanished thence, sad and dejected.

5. Uppalavaṇṇā.

Now, Bhikkhunī Uppalavaṇṇā ... entered the Dark Wood
for siesta, and, plunging into its depths, halted at the root of a
certain sāla-tree in full blossom. Then Māra ... addressed her in a
verse:

'Thou that art come where over thee crowned with blossom
[Waveth] the sāl-tree, Sister, and standest alone in the shade of it,
No one like thee could hither come rival to beauty as thine is !
Fearest thou not, O foolish maiden, the wiles of seducers ?'

Then Bhikkhunī Uppalavaṇṇā thought ... 'Sure 'tis Māra !'
... and replied with verses:

'Were there an hundred thousand seducers e'en such as thou art,
Ne'er would I tremble affrighted thereat, or turn a hair of me.
Māra, I fear not thee, all lonely though I be standing.
Here though I stand, I vanish, or enter into thy body.
See ! 'twixt thine eyelashes hide, standing where thou canst not
see me.
For all my mind is wholly self-controlled,
And the Four Paths to Potency are thoroughly learnt.
Yea, I am free from all the Bonds there be.
In sooth, good sir, no fear have I of thee !'

Then Māra, thinking, 'Bhikkhunī Uppalavaṇṇā knows me !'
vanished thence, sad and dejected.

6. Cālā.

Now, Bhikkhunī Cālā.... sat down at the root of a certain
tree for siesta. Then Māra the Evil One went up to her, and spoke
thus to her: 'Wherein, O Sister, dost thou find no pleasure ?'
'In birth, good sir, I find no pleasure.'
'Why findest thou no pleasure in birth ? Once born, one
enjoys the pleasures of a life of sense. Who hath put this into thy
mind, "Find no pleasure in birth", Sister ?'

'Once born, we die. Once born, we see life's Ills —
The bonds, the torments, and the life cut off.
The Buddha hath revealed the Norm to us —
How we may get beyond the power of birth,
How we may put an end to every Ill.
'Tis He hath guided me into the True.
They who have come to worlds of Form, and they
Who in those worlds abide where Form is not,
An they know not how they may end it all,
Are goers, all of them, again to birth.'

Then Māra, thinking, 'Bhikkhunī Cālā knows me !'
vanished thence, sad and dejected.

7. Upacālā.

Now, Bhikkhunī Upacālā ... sat down at the root of a
certain tree for siesta.

Then Māra the Evil One, desiring to arouse fear ... to make
her desist from concentrated thought, went up to her, and spoke
thus to her:

'Where, Sister, dost thou wish to rise again ?'

'Nowhere, good sir, I wish to rise again.'

'Now, think upon the Three-and-Thirty gods,
And on the gods who rule in realm of Shades,
On those who reign in Heaven of Bliss, and on
Those higher deities who live where life
Yet flows by way of sense and of desire —
Think, and thither aspire with longing heart,

The bliss of each in turn shall then be thine.'

Upacālā

'Ay, think upon the Three-and-Thirty gods,
And on the gods who rule in realm of Shades,
On those who reign in Heaven of Bliss, and on
Those higher deities who live where life
Yet flows by way of sense and of desire !
They all are bound by bonds of sense-desire,
Hence come they evermore 'neath Māra's sway.
On fire is all the world, is wrapt in smoke.
Ablaze is all the world, the heav'ns do quake !
But that which quaketh not, influctuate,
Untrodden by the average worldling's feet,
Where Māra cometh not nor hath way-gate —
There doth my heart abide in blest retreat.'

Then Māra, thinking, 'Bhikkhunī Upacālā knows me !' vanished thence, sad and dejected.

8. Sīsupacālā.

Now, Bhikkhunī Sīsupacālā ... sat down at the root of a certain tree for siesta.

Then Māra the Evil One went up to her, and spoke to her thus: 'Of whose shibboleth, Sister, dost thou approve ?'

'I approve of no one's shibboleth, good sir.'

'Why now and whereto art thou seen thus garbed
And shaven like a nun, yet dost not join
Ascetics of some sort and shibboleth ?

What, futile and infatuate, is thy quest ?'

''Tis they that are without, caught in the net
Of the vain shibboleths in which they trust —
Their's is the doctrine I cannot approve.
'Tis they that lack acquaintance with the Norm.

Lo ! in the princely Sākiya clan is born
A Buddha peerless 'mong the sons of men,
Who all hath overcome, before whose face
Māra doth flee away, who everywhere
Unconquered stands, He that is wholly freed
And fetterless, the Seer who seeth all,
For whom all karma is destroyed, who in
The perishing of every germ that birth
Once more engenders, is at liberty.
This the Exalted One, my Master and my Lord:
His doctrine, His the word that I approve.'

Then Māra, thinking, 'Bhikkhunī Sīsupacālā knows me !'
vanished thence, sad and dejected.

9. Selā.

Now, Bhikkhunī Selā ... sat down at the root of a certain
tree for siesta.
Then Māra ... went up to her, and addressed her with a
verse:

'Who was't that made this human puppet's form ?
Where, tell me, is the human doll's artificer ?
Whence hath the human puppet come to be ?
Where, tell me, shall it cease and pass away ?'

Then Bhikkhunī Selā thought ... 'Sure 'tis Māra !'... and replied with verses:

'Neither self-made the puppet is, nor yet
By other is this evil fashioned.
By reason of a cause it came to be;
By rupture of a cause, it dies away.
Like to a given seed sown in the field,
Which, when it lighteth on the taste of earth
And moisture likewise, by these twain doth grow,
So the five aggregates, the elements,
And the six spheres of sense — even all these —
By reason of a cause they came to be;
By rupture of a cause they die away.'

Then Māra, thinking, 'Bhikkhunī Selā knows me!' vanished thence, sad and dejected.

10. Vajirā.

Now Bhikkhunī Vajirā ... sat down at the root of a certain tree for siesta.

Then Māra ... went up to her, and addressed her with a verse:

'Who hath this being fashioned ? Where is
The maker of this being ? Whence hath it sprung ?
Where doth this being cease and pass away ?'

Then Bhikkhunī Vajirā thought ... 'Sure 'tis Māra !'' ... and replied with a verse:

'"Being"? Why dost thou harp upon that word?
'Mong false opinions, Māra, art thou strayed.
This a mere bundle of formations is.
Therefrom no "being" mayest thou obtain.
For e'en as, when the factors are arranged,
The product by the word "chariot" is known,
So doth our usage covenant to say
"A being", when the aggregates are there.
'Tis simply Ill that riseth, simply Ill
That doth persist, and then fadeth away.
Nought beside Ill it is that doth become;
Nought else but Ill it is doth pass away.'

Then Māra, thinking, 'Bhikkhunī Vajirā knows me!'
vanished thence, sad and dejected.

Here endeth the Bhikkhunī Series.

THERĪGĀTHĀ

SINGLE VERSES

A certain unknown bhikkhunī

1. Sleep happily, little therī, clad in the garment which you have made; for your desire is stilled, like dried-up vegetables in a pot.

Muttā

2. Muttā, be freed from ties, as the moon, when grasped by Rāhu, is freed; with mind completely freed, without debt, enjoy your alms-food.

Puṇṇā

3. Puṇṇā, be filled with good mental states, as full as the moon on the 15th day; with fulfilled wisdom tear asunder the mass of darkness (of ignorance).

Tissā

4. Tissā, be trained in the training; may the opportune occasions not pass you by. Unfettered from all ties, live in the world without āsavas.

Another Tissā

5. Tissā, apply yourself to good mental states; do not let the opportune moment pass you by. For those who have missed the opportune moment grieve when consigned to hell.

Dhīrā

6. Dhīrā, attain cessation, the stilling of evil notions, happiness; gain quenching, unsurpassed rest-from-exertion.

Another Dhīrā

7. You are Dhīrā because of your firm (*dhīra*) mental states; you are a bhikkhunī with developed faculties. Bear your last body, having conquered Māra and his mount.

(not reborn is monk)

Mittā

8. Mittā, having gone forth in faith, be one who delights in friends (*mitta*); develop good mental states for the attainment of rest-from-exertion.

Bhadrā

9. Bhadrā, having gone forth in faith, be one who delights in auspicious things (*bhadra*); develop good mental states, and unsurpassed rest-from-exertion.

Upasamā

10. Upasamā, you should cross the flood, the realm of death which is very hard to cross. Bear your last body, having conquered Māra and his mount.

Muttā

11. I am well-released, properly released by my release by means of the three crooked things, by the mortar, pestle, and my crooked husband. I am released from birth and death; everything which leads to renewed existence has been rooted out.

Dhammadinnā

12. One should be eager, determinate, and suffused with mind; one whose thought is not attached to sensual pleasures is called an "up-streamer".

Visākhā

13. Do the Buddha's teaching; having done it one does not repent; wash your feet quickly, and sit down on one side.

Sumanā

14. Seeing the elements as pain, do not come to birth again; discarding desire for existence, you will wander, stilled.

Uttarā

15. I was restrained in body, speech, and mind. I have plucked out craving root and all, and have become cool, quenched.

Sumanā, who went forth when old

16. Lie down happily, old lady, clad in the garment which you have made; for your desire is stilled; you have become cool, quenched.

Dhammā

17. I wandered for alms, leaning on a stick, weak; with trembling limbs I fell to the ground in that very spot. Seeing peril in the body, then my mind was completely released.

Saṅghā

18. Giving up my house, gone forth, giving up son, cattle, and whatever was dear to me, giving up desire and hatred, and discarding ignorance, plucking out craving root and all, I have become stilled, quenched.

PAIRS OF VERSES

Nandā

19. Nandā, see the body, diseased, impure, rotten; develop the mind, intent and well-concentrated, for contemplation of the unpleasant.
20. And develop the signless, cast out the latent tendency to conceit. Then by the full understanding of conceit, you will wander, stilled.

Jentī

21. I have developed all these seven constituents of enlightenment, the ways for the attainment of quenching, as taught by the Buddha.
22. I have indeed seen that blessed one; this is the last body; journeying-on from rebirth to rebirth has been completely annihilated; there is now no renewed existence.

A certain unknown bhikkhunī

23. I am well-released, well-released, properly released from the pestle. My shameless man, even his sun-shade, etc., disgust me. My pot gives forth the smell of water-snake.
24. I destroy desire and hatred with a sizzling sound. I go up to the foot of a tree, and thinking "O the happiness", meditate upon it as happiness.

Aḍḍhakāsī

25. My wages of prostitution were as large as the revenue of the country of Kāsi; the townspeople fixed that price and made me priceless in price.

26. Then I became disgusted with my beauty, and being disgusted I was disinterested in it. May I not run again through the journeying-on from rebirth to rebirth again and again. I have realized the three knowledges. I have done the Buddha's teaching

Cittā

27. Although I am thin, sick, and very weak, I go along leaning on a stick, having climbed the mountain.

28. I threw down my outer robe, and turned my bowl upside down; I propped myself against a rock, tearing asunder the mass of darkness (of ignorance).

Mettikā

29. Although I am pained, weak, with my youth gone, I go along leaning on a stick, having climbed the mountain.

30. I threw down my outer robe, and turned my bowl upside down. I sat down on a rock. Then my mind was completely released. I have obtained the three knowledges. I have done the Buddha's teaching.

Mittā

31. The 14th, the 15th, and the 8th day of the fortnight, and a special day of the fortnight, I kept as a fast-day, which is well-connected with the eight-fold precepts. I longed for rebirth in a

connected with the eight-fold precepts. I longed for rebirth in a divine group.

32. Today with a single meal each day, with shaven head, clad in the outer robe, I do not wish for rebirth in a divine group. I have removed the fear in my heart.

˙Abhayamātā

33. Mother, from the soles of the feet upwards, from the head and hair downwards, consider this impure, evil-smelling body.

34. As I dwell in this way all my desire has been rooted out; the burning fever has been cut out; I have become cool, quenched.

Abhayattherī

35. Abhayā, fragile is the body, to which ordinary individuals are attached. Attentive and possessed of mindfulness, I shall discard this body.

36. Delighting in vigilance because of many painful objects, I have obtained the annihilation of craving. I have done the Buddha's teaching.

Sāmā

37. Four or five times I went out from my cell, not having obtained peace of mind, being without self-mastery over the mind.

38. This is the eighth night since my craving was completely rooted out. Delighting in vigilance because of many painful objects, I have obtained the annihilation of craving. I have done

objects, I have obtained the annihilation of craving. I have done the Buddha's teaching.

GROUPS OF THREE VERSES

Another Sāmā

39. Twenty-five years have passed since I went forth. I am not aware of having obtained peace of mind at any time.

40. Without peace of mind, without self-mastery over the mind, then I reached a state of religious excitement, remembering the teaching of the conqueror.

41. Delighting in vigilance because of many painful objects, I have obtained the annihilation of craving. I have done the Buddha's teaching. Today is the seventh day since my craving was dried up.

Uttamā

42. Four or five times I went out from my cell, not having obtained peace of mind, being without self-mastery over the mind.

43. I went up to a bhikkhunī who was fit to be trusted by me. She taught me the doctrine, the elements of existence, the sense-bases, and the elements.

44. I heard the doctrine from her as she instructed me; for seven days I sat in one and the same cross-legged position, consigned to joy and happiness. On the eighth day I stretched forth my feet, having torn asunder the mass of darkness (of ignorance).

Another Uttamā

45. I have developed all these seven constituents of enlightenment, the ways for the obtaining of quenching, as taught by the Buddha.

46. I am an attainer of the empty, or the signless aspects of nibbāna, whichever is wanted. I am the true daughter of the Buddha, always delighting in quenching.

47. All sensual pleasures, those which are divine and those which are human, have been completely cut out. Journeying-on from rebirth to rebirth has been completely annihilated; there is now no renewed existence.

Dantikā

48. Going out from my daytime-resting-place on Mt. Gijjhakūṭa, I saw an elephant on the bank of the river, having come up after plunging in.

49. A man, taking a hook, requested the elephant, "Give me your foot." The elephant stretched forth its foot; the man mounted the elephant.

50. Seeing the untamed tamed, gone under the control of men, I then concentrated my mind, gone to the forest for that purpose indeed.

Ubbirī

51. Mother, you cry out "O Jīva" in the wood; understand yourself, Ubbirī. 84,000 daughters, all with the name Jīva, have been burned in this funeral fire. Which of these do you

have been burned in this funeral fire. Which of these do you
grieve for ?

52. Truly he has plucked out my dart, hard to see, nestling in my
heart, which grief for my daughter he has thrust away for me,
overcome by grief.

53. Today I have my dart plucked out; I am without hunger,
quenched. I go to the Buddha-sage, the doctrine, and the Order
as a refuge.

Sukkā

54. What has happened to these men in Rājagaha ? They remain as
though they have drunk wine. They do not attend upon Sukkā
when she is preaching the Buddha's teaching.

55. But the wise drink the teaching, I think, which is not
repellent, never causing surfeit, of sweet flavour, as travellers
drink a rain-cloud.

56. You are Sukkā because of your bright (sukka) mental states,
being rid of desire, concentrated. Bear your last body, having
conquered Māra and his mount.

Selā

57. There is no escape in the world; what will you do with
seclusion ? Enjoy the delights of sensual pleasures; do not
repent afterwards.

58. Sensual pleasures are like swords and stakes; the elements of
existence are a chopping block for them; what you call "delight
in sensual pleasures" is now "non-delight" for me.

59. Everywhere enjoyment of pleasure is defeated; the mass of darkness (of ignorance) is torn asunder; in this way know, evil one, you are defeated, death.

Somā

60. That place, hard to gain, which is to be attained by the seers, cannot be attained by a woman with two-finger-intelligence (= very little intelligence).

61. What harm could the woman's state do to us, when the mind is well-concentrated, when knowledge exists for someone rightly having insight into the doctrine ?

62. Everywhere enjoyment of pleasure is defeated; the mass of darkness (of ignorance) is torn asunder; in this way know, evil one, you are defeated, death.

THE GROUP OF FOUR VERSES

Bhaddā Kāpilānī

63. Kassapa, the son, the heir of the Buddha, well-concentrated, who knows that he has lived before, and sees heaven and hell,

64. and has attained the destruction of rebirths, is a sage perfected in supernormal knowledge. Because of these three knowledges he is a brahman with triple knowledge.

65. In just the same way Bhaddā Kāpilānī, with triple knowledge, having left death behind, bears her last body, having conquered Māra and his mount. *Comparison w/ Exalted Man*

66. Having seen the peril in the world, we both went forth; with āsavas annihilated, tamed, we have become cool, quenched.

GROUPS OF FIVE VERSES

A certain unknown bhikkhunī

67. It is 25 years since I went forth. Not even for the duration of a snap of the fingers have I obtained stilling of the mind.
68. Not obtaining peace of mind, drenched with desire for sensual pleasures, holding out my arms, crying out, I entered the vihāra.
69. I went up to a bhikkhunī who was fit to be trusted by me. She taught me the doctrine, the elements of existence, the sense-bases, and the elements.
70. I heard the doctrine from her, and sat down on one side. I know that I have lived before; I have purified the divine eye;
71. and there is knowledge of the state of mind of others; I have purified the ear-element; I have realized supernormal power too; I have attained the annihilation of the āsavas; I have realized these six supernormal knowledges; I have done the Buddha's teaching.

Vimalā, the former courtesan

72. Intoxicated by my good complexion, my figure, beauty, and fame, haughty because of my youth, I despised other women.
73. Having decorated this body, very variegated, deceiving fools, I stood at the brothel door, like a hunter having spread out a snare,
74. showing my ornamentation. Many a secret place was revealed. I did various sorts of conjuring, mocking many people.
75. Today I have wandered for alms with shaven head, clad in the outer robe, and am seated at the foot of a tree; I have obtained the stage of non-reasoning.

76. I have cut out all ties, those which are divine and those which are human. I have annihilated all the āsavas; I have become cool, quenched.

Sīhā

77. Afflicted by desire for sensual pleasures, because of unreasoned thinking, previously I was conceited, being without self-mastery over the mind.

78. Obsessed by the defilements, giving way to the notion of happiness, I did not obtain peace of mind, being under the influence of thoughts of passion.

79. Thin, pale, and wan, I wandered for seven years; being very pained, I did not find happiness by day or night.

80. Then taking a rope, I went into a wood, thinking "It is better to hang myself than to lead a low life again."

81. I made a strong noose, and tied it to the branch of a tree. I cast the noose around my neck. Then my mind was completely released.

Nandā

82. "See the body, Nandā, disease, impure, rotten. Devote the mnd, intent and well-concentrated, to contemplation of the unpleasant.

83. As this is, so is that; as that is, so is this. It gives out a rotten evil smell, it is what fools delight in."

84. Looking at it in this way, not relaxing day or night, then analysing it by my own wisdom, I saw.

85. Reflecting in a reasoned manner, I saw this body as it really was, inside and out.

86. Then I became disgusted with the body, and I was disinterested internally. Vigilant, unfettered, I have become stilled, quenched.

Nanduttarā

87. I used to worship fire, and the moon, and the sun, and divinities. I went to river-fording places, and used to go down into the water.

88. Undertaking many vows, I shaved half my head; I made my bed on the ground; I did not eat night-food.

89. Delighting in ornament and decoration, by means of bathing and anointing indeed, I ministered to this body, afflicted by desire for sensual pleasure.

90. Then obtaining faith I went forth into the houseless state, seeing the body as it really was. I have rooted out desire for sensual pleasures.

91. I have cut out all existences, and wishes and longings too. Unfettered from all ties, I have attained peace of mind.

Mittakālī

92. I went forth in faith from the house to the houseless state, and wandered here and there, greedy for gain and honour.

93. I missed the highest goal, and pursued the lowest goal. Gone under the mastery of the defilements, I did not know the goal of the ascetic's state.

94. I experienced religious excitement, as I sat in my little cell; thinking "I have enterted upon the wrong road: I have come under the mastery of craving.

95. My life is short. Old age and sickness are destroying it. There is no time for me to be careless before this body is broken."

96. Looking at the arising and passing away of the elements of existence as they really are, I stood up with my mind completely released. I have done the Buddha's teaching.

Sakulā

97. Living in a house, I heard the doctrine from a bhikkhu, and saw the stainless doctrine, quenching, the unshaken state.

98. I abandoned son and daughter, and money and grain; I had my hair cut off, and went forth into the houseless state.

99. Undergoing training, developing the straight way, I eliminated desire and hatred, and the āsavas which are combined with these.

100. I was ordained as a bhikkhunī, and recollected that I had been born before. The divine eye has been purified; it is spotless, well-developed.

101. Seeing the constituent elements as other, arisen causally, liable to dissolution, I eliminated all āsavas; I have become cool, quenched.

Soṇā

102. I bore ten sons in this material body, and then being weak and aged I approached a bhikkhunī.

103. She taught me the doctrine, the elements of existence, the sense-bases, and the elements. When I heard the doctrine from her, I cut off my hair, and went forth.

104. As I underwent training the divine eye was purified. I know my former habitation, in which I had lived before.

105. And, intent and well concentrated, I develop the signless. I have had immediate complete release; I have become quenched without clinging.

106. When they are known, the five elements of existence stand with root cut off. Born from an enduring foundation, I am immovable. There is now no renewed existence.

Bhaddā, the former Jain

107. With hair cut off, wearing dust, formerly I wandered, having only one robe, thinking there was a fault where there was no fault, and seeing no fault where there was a fault.

108. Going out from my daytime resting-place on Mt. Gijjhakūṭa, I saw the stainless Buddha, attended by the Order of bhikkhus.

109. Having bent the knee, having paid homage to him, I stood with cupped hands face to face with him. "Come, Bhaddā," he said to me; that was my ordination.

110. I have wandered over Aṅga, and Magadha, Vajjī, Kāsi, and Kosala. For 50 years without debt I have enjoyed the alms of the kingdoms.

111. Truly he produced much merit; truly wise was that lay-follower who gave a robe to Bhaddā who is now freed from all bonds.

Paṭācārā

112. Ploughing the field with ploughs, sowing seeds in the ground, nourishing wives and children, young brahmans find wealth.

113. Why do I, possessed of virtuous conduct, complying with [FRUSTRATION] the teaching of the teacher, not obtain quenching ? I am not slack, nor puffed-up.

114. I washed my feet, and paid attention to the waters; and seeing the foot-water come flowing downhill from the high land to the low land, then I concentrated my mind, like a noble thoroughbred horse.

115. Then I took a lamp and I entered my cell. I inspected the bed, and sat on the couch.

116. Then I took a needle and drew out the wick. The complete release of my mind was like the quenching of the lamp.

Thirty bhikkhunīs

117. "Having taken pestles, young brahmans grind corn; nourishing wives and children, young brahmans find wealth.

118. Do the Buddha's teaching; having done it one does not repent. Wash your feet quickly, and sit down on one side. Intent on peace of mind, do the Buddha's teaching."

119. They heard her utterance, Paṭācārā's teaching; they washed [WOMAN] their feet, and sat down on one side. Intent on peace of mind, [TEACHER] they did the Buddha's teaching.

120. In the first watch of the night they recollected that they had been born before; in the middle watch of the night they purified [STUDENTS] the divine eye; in the last watch of the night they tore asunder [LIKE BUDDHA] the mass of darkness (of ignorance).

121. Standing up they paid homage to her feet. "We have taken your advice; we shall dwell honouring you like the 30 deities honouring Inda, who is unconquered in battle. We have the triple knowledge; we are without āsavas."

Candā

122. Formerly I fared ill, a widow, without children. Without
     friends and relations I did not obtain food or clothing.
123. Taking a bowl and stick, begging from family to family, and
     being burned by cold and heat, I wandered for seven years.
124. But then I saw a bhikkhunī who had obtained food and drink,
     and approaching her I said, "Send me forth into the houseless
     state."
125. And Patācārā, in pity, sent me forth; then she exhorted me,
     and urged me towards the highest goal.
126. I heard her utterance and took her advice. The noble lady's
     exhortation was not in vain; I have the triple knowledge; I am
     without āsavas.

GROUPS OF SIX VERSES

Pañcasatā Paṭācārā

PAṬĀCĀRĀ'S TEACHING

127. "Whose way you do not know, either coming or going, that being you lament, come from who knows where, crying 'My son.' *GRIEF FOR SON*

128. But you do not grieve for him whose way you do know, either coming or going; for such is the nature of living creatures.

129. Unasked he came from there, unpermitted he went from here, surely having come from somewhere or other, having lived a few days.

130. He went from here by one road, he will go from there by another. Passed away with the form of a man he will go journeying-on. As he came, so he went. What lamentation is there in that ?"

131. Truly she has plucked out my dart, hard to see, nestling in my heart; she has thrust away that grief for my son for me, overcome by grief.

132. Today I have my dart plucked out; I am without hunger, quenched. I go to the Buddha-sage, the doctrine, and the Order, as a refuge.

Vāsiṭṭhī

133. Afflicted by grief for my son, with mind deranged, out of my senses, naked, and with dishevelled hair, I wandered here and there.

134. I dwelt on rubbish heaps in the streets, in a cemetery, and on highways; I wandered for three years, consigned to hunger and thirst.

135. Then I saw the well-farer who had gone to the city of Mithilā, the tamer of the untamed, the enlightened one, who has no fear from any quarter.

136. Regaining my mind, I paid homage to him, and sat down. In pity Gotama taught me the doctrine.

137. I heard the doctrine from him, and went forth into the houseless state. Applying myself to the teacher's utterance, I realized the blissful state.

138. All griefs have been cut out, eliminated, ending in this way; for I have comprehended the grounds, from which is the origin of griefs.

Khemā

139. "You are young and beautiful; I also am young and in my prime. Come, Khemā, let us delight ourselves with the 5-fold music."

140. I am afflicted by and ashamed of this foul body, diseased, perishable. Craving for sensual pleasures has been rooted out.

141. Sensual pleasures are like swords and stakes; the elements of existence are a chopping block for them; what you call "delight in sensual pleasures" is now "non-delight" for me.

142. Everywhere love of pleasure is defeated; the mass of darkness (of ignorance) is torn asunder; in this way know, evil one, you are defeated, death.

143. Revering the lunar mansions, tending the fire in the wood, not knowing it as it really is, fools, you thought it was purity.

144. But revering the enlightened one, best of men, I am indeed completely released from all pains, doing the teacher's teaching.

Sujātā

145. Ornamented, well-dressed, wearing a garland smeared with sandalwood-paste, covered with all my ornaments, attended by a crowd of slave-women, *RICH LADY*

146. taking food and drink, food hard and soft, in no small quantity, going out from the house I betook myself to the pleasure garden.

147. Having delighted there, having played, coming back to my own house, I saw a vihāra. I entered the Añjana wood at Sāketa. *HEARS BS TEACHING*

148. I saw the light of the world. I paid homage to him and sat down. In pity the one with vision taught me the doctrine.

149. And hearing the great seer, I completely pierced the truth. In that very place I attained the stainless doctrine, the state of the undying.

150. Then knowing the true doctrine, I went forth into the houseless state. I have obtained the three knowledges; the Buddha's teaching was not in vain.

Anopamā

151. I was born in an exalted family, which had much property and much wealth. I possessed a good complexion and figure, being Majjha's own daughter. *RICH + BEAUTIFUL LADY*

152. I was sought after by kings' sons, longed for by merchants' sons; one sent my father a messenger, saying "Give me Anopamā.

153. However much that daughter of yours Anopamā weighs, I will give you eight times that amount of gold and jewels."

154. I saw the enlightened one, who was supreme in the world, unsurpassed. I paid homage to his feet, and sat down on one side.

155. In pity Gotama taught me the doctrine. Seated on that seat I attained the third fruit.

156. Then I cut off my hair and went forth into the houseless state. Today is the seventh night since my craving was dried up.

Mahāpajāpatī Gotamī

157. Buddha, hero, homage to you, best of all creatures, who released me and many other people from pain.

158. All pain is known; craving as the cause is dried up; the noble eight-fold way has been developed; I have attained cessation.

159. Formerly I was mother, son, father, brother, and grandmother; not having proper knowledge, I journeyed-on without expiation.

160. I have indeed seen that blessed one; this is the last body; journeying-on from rebirth to rebirth has been completely eliminated; there is now no renewed existence.

161. I see the disciples all together, putting forth energy, resolute, always with strong effort; this is homage to the Buddhas.

162. Truly Māyā bore Gotama for the sake of many. He has thrust away the mass of pain of those struck by sickness and death.

Guttā

163. Guttā, give up your son, and those who are equally dear to you, and devote yourself to that very thing for the sake of which you went forth. Do not go under the influence of mind.

164. Creatures, deceived by mind, delighting in Māra's realm, run through the journeying-on of numerous rebirths, ignorant.

165. Desire for sensual pleasures, and malevolence, and the false view of individuality, misapprehension about rules of virtuous conduct and vows, and uncertainty fifth —

166. bhikkhunī, abandoning these fetters, which lead to the lower-world, you will not come to this again.

167. Avoiding desire, pride, and ignorance, and conceit, cutting the fetters, you will put an end to pain.

168. Annihilating journeying-on from rebirth to rebirth, comprehending and giving up renewed existence, you will wander in the world of phenomena, without hunger, stilled.

Vijayā

169. Four or five times I went forth from my cell, not having obtained peace of mind, being without self-mastery over the mind.

170. I approached a bhikkhunī, honoured her, and questioned (her). She taught me the doctrine, and the elements, and sense-bases,

171. the four noble truths, the faculties, and the powers, the constituents of enlightenment and the eight-fold way for the attainment of the supreme goal.

172. I heard her utterance, took her advice, and in the first watch of the night I recollected that I had been born before.

173. In the middle watch of the night I purified the divine eye. In the last watch of the night I tore asunder the mass of darkness (of ignorance).

174. And I then dwelt suffusing the body with joy and happiness. On the seventh day I stretched forth my feet, having torn asunder the mass of darkness (of ignorance).

GROUPS OF SEVEN VERSES

Uttarā

175. "Young brahmans take pestles and grind corn; nourishing wives and children, young brahmans find wealth.

176. Strive after the Buddha's teaching; having done it one does not repent. Wash your feet quickly, and sit down on one side.

177. Summoning up the mind, intent and well-concentrated, consider the constituent elements as other, and not as self."

178. Having heard her utterance, the advice of Paṭācārā, having washed my feet, I sat down on one side.

179. In the first watch of the night I recollected that I had been born before; in the middle watch of the night I purified the divine eye;

180. in the last watch of the night I tore asunder the mass of darkness (of ignorance). Then I stood up with the triple knowledge. Your advice has been taken.

181. I shall dwell honouring you like the 30 deities honouring Inda, who is unconquered in battle. I have the triple knowledge; I am without āsavas.

Cālā

182. Summoning up mindfulness, a bhikkhunī with developed faculties, I pierced the peaceful state, the stilling of the constituent elements, happiness.

183. "Following whose teaching have you shaved your head ? You seem like an ascetic, but you do not approve of sectarians. Why do you practise this, being foolish ?"

184. Sectarians outside this Order rely upon false views. They do not know the doctrine; they are not proficient in the doctrine.

185. The Buddha, the unrivalled one, was born in the Sakya clan. He taught me the doctrine, the complete overcoming of false views:—

186. pain, the uprising of pain, and the overcoming of pain, the noble eight-fold way leading to the stilling of pain.

187. I heard his utterance, and dwelt delighting in his teaching. I have obtained the three knowledges. I have done the Buddha's teaching.

188. Everywhere the enjoyment of pleasure is defeated; the mass of darkness (of ignorance) is torn asunder; in this way know, evil one, you are defeated, death.

Upacālā

189. Possessed of mindfulness, possessed of vision, a bhikkhunī with developed faculties, I pierced the peaceful state, which is not cultivated by evil men.

190. "Why do you not approve of birth ? Anyone who is born enjoys sensual pleasures. Enjoy the delights of sensual pleasures; do not repent afterwards."

191. For anyone who is born there is death, the cutting-off of hands and feet, slaughter, bonds, and calamity. Anyone who is born goes to pain.

192. The unconquered enlightened one was born in the Sakya clan. He taught me the doctrine, the complete overcoming of birth:—

193. pain, the uprising of pain, and the overcoming of pain, the noble eight-fold way leading to the stilling of pain.

194. I heard his utterance, and I dwelt delighting in his teaching. I have obtained the three knowledges. I have done the Buddha's teaching.

195. Everywhere the enjoyment of pleasure is defeated; the mass
of darkness (of ignorance) is torn asunder; in this way know,
evil one, you are defeated, death.

THE GROUP OF EIGHT VERSES

Sīsûpacālā

196. A bhikkhunī, possessed of virtue, well-controlled in her faculties, should obtain the peaceful state, never causing surfeit, of sweet flavour.

197. "The Tāvatiṃsa, and Yāma, and Tusita divinities, the Nimmānarati deities, and the Vasavatti deities; apply your mind there, where you lived before."

198. The Tāvatiṃsa, and Yāma, and Tusita divinities, the Nimmānarati deities, and the Vasavatti deities,

199. again and again, from existence to existence, are exposed to individuality, not passing beyond individuality, going to birth and death.

200. The whole world is ablaze, the whole world has flared up, the whole world is blazing, the whole world is shaken.

201. The Buddha taught me the doctrine, unshakable, incomparable, not cultivated by ordinary people. My mind was deeply attached to it.

202. I heard his utterance, and I dwelt delighting in his teaching. I have obtained the three knowledges. I have done the Buddha's teaching.

203. Everywhere the enjoyment of pleasure is defeated; the mass of darkness (of ignorance) is torn asunder; in this way know, evil one, you are defeated, death.

THE GROUP OF NINE VERSES

Vaḍḍha's mother

[handwritten margin note: MOTHER → DAUGHTER]

204. "May you not have, Vaḍḍha, craving for the world at any time. Child, do not share in pain again and again.

205. The sages dwell happily indeed, Vaḍḍha, free from lust, with doubts cut off, become cool, having attained self-taming, being without āsavas.

206. Vaḍḍha, devote yourself to the way practised by those seers for the attainment of insight, for the putting of an end to pain."

207. "Confident indeed you speak this matter to me, mother. Now indeed, I think, craving is not found in you, mother."

208. "Whatever constituent elements, Vaḍḍha, are low, high, or middle, no craving, even minute, even of minute size, for them is found in me."

209. "All my āsavas have been annihilated as I meditate, vigilant. I have obtained the three knowledges. I have done the Buddha's teaching.

210. Truly my mother, because she was sympathetic, applied an excellent goad to me, namely verses connected with the highest goal. I heard her utterance, my mother's instruction, and I reached a state of religious excitement in the doctrine, for the attainment of rest-from-exertion.

212. Being resolute for exertion, not relaxing day or night, urged on by my mother, I attained supreme peace."

THE GROUP OF ELEVEN VERSES

Kisāgotamī

213. The state of having noble friends has been praised by the sage with reference to the world; if he resorted to noble friends, even a fool would be wise.

214. Good men are to be resorted to; in this way the wisdom of those who resort to them increases. Resorting to good men one would be released from all pains.

215. One should know pain, and the uprising of pain, and its cessation, and the eight-fold way, even the four noble truths.

216. The state of women has been said to be painful by the charioteer of men who are to be tamed; even the state of being a co-wife is painful; some, having given birth once, *pains of labor...*

217. even cut their throats; some tender ones take poisons; considered as murderers in hell both groups suffer misfortunes.

218. Going along, about to bring forth, I saw my husband dead; having given birth on the path, I had not yet arrived at my own house.

219. Two sons dead and a husband dead upon the path for miserable me; mother and father and brother were burning upon one pyre. *whole family dies*

220. Miserable woman, with family annihilated, you have suffered immeasurable pain; and you have shed tears for many thousands of births.

221. Then I saw the flesh of my sons being eaten in the midst of the cemetery; with my family destroyed, despised by all, with husband dead, I attained the undying.

222. I have developed the noble eight-fold way leading to the undying; I have realized quenching; I have looked at the doctrine as a mirror.

223. I have my dart cut out, my burden laid down; I have done that which was to be done. The therī Kisāgotamī, with mind completely released, has said this.

THE GROUP OF TWELVE VERSES

Uppalavaṇṇā

224. The two of us, mother and daughter, were co-wives; I experienced religious excitement, amazing, hair-raising.

225. Woe upon sensual pleasures, impure, evil-smelling, with many troubles, wherein we, mother and daughter, were co-wives.

226. I saw the peril in sensual pleasures, and I saw renunciation of the world as firm security; I went forth at Rājagaha from the house to the houseless state.

227. I know that I have lived before; I have purified the divine eye; and there is knowledge of the state of mind of others; I have purified the ear-element;

228. I have realized supernormal power too; I have attained the annihilation of the āsavas: I have realized these six supernormal knowledges; I have done the Buddha's teaching.

229. I fashioned a four-horsed chariot by supernormal power, paid homage to the Buddha's feet, the glorious protector of the world, and I stood on one side.

230. "Going up to a tree with well-flowered top, you stand there alone at the foot of the tree; you do not even have a companion; child, are you not afraid of rogues ?"

231. Even if 100,000 rogues like you were to come together, I should not move a hair's breadth, I should not even shake. What will you alone do to me, Māra ?

232. I shall disappear, or I shall enter into your belly; I shall stand between your eyebrows; you will not see me standing there.

233. I have mastery over my mind; I have developed the bases of supernormal power well; I have realized the six supernormal knowledges. I have done the Buddha's teaching.

234. Sensual pleasures are like swords and stakes; the elements of existence are a chopping block for them; what you call "delight in sensual pleasures" is now "non-delight" for me.

235. Everywhere enjoyment of pleasure is defeated; the mass of darkness (of ignorance) is torn asunder; in this way know, evil one, you are defeated, death.

THE GROUP OF SIXTEEN VERSES

Puṇṇikā

CONVERSION OF A BARNST BRAHMIN

236. "I am a <u>water-carrier</u>; even in the cold weather I have always gone down to the water, terrified by fear of punishment from noble ladies, harrassed by fear of abuse and displeasure.

237. What are *you* afraid of, brahman, when you constantly go down to the water ? With trembling limbs you experience very great cold."

238. "But you already know the answer, lady Puṇṇikā; you ask one who is doing good action, and thereby blocking off evil action.

239. Whoever, whether young or old, does an evil action, even he is released from his evil action by ablution in water."

240. "Who indeed told you this, ignorant to the ignorant: 'Truly he is released from his evil action by ablution in water ?"

241. Now if this is true all frogs and turtles will go to heaven, and alligators and crocodiles and the other water-dwellers.

242. Sheep-butchers, pork-butchers, fishermen, animal-trappers, thieves and executioners, and other evil-doers, even they will be released from their evil action by ablution in water.

243. If these streams carried away the evil you had previously done, they would carry away your merit too; thereby you would be devoid of both.

244. Do not do the very thing, brahman, for fear of which you have always gone down to the water; brahman, do not let the cold strike your skin."

245. "Noble lady, you have brought me, entered upon the wrong way, back into the noble way. I give you this water-ablution robe."

246. "Keep the robe for yourself; I do not want the robe; if you are afraid of pain, if pain is unpleasant for you,

247. do not do an evil action either openly or in secret. But if you do or will do an evil action,

248. there is no release from pain for you, even if you fly up and run away. If you are afraid of pain, if pain is unpleasant for you,

249. go to the venerable Buddha as a refuge, to the doctrine, and to the Order; undertake the rules of virtuous conduct; that will be to your advantage."

250. "I go to the venerable Buddha as a refuge, to the doctrine, and to the Order; I undertake the rules of virtuous conduct; that will be to my advantage.

251. Formerly I was a kinsman of Brahmā; today I am truly a brahman. I possess the triple knowledge, I am endowed with knowledge, and I am versed in sacred lore; and I am washed clean."

GROUPS OF TWENTY VERSES

Ambapālī

OLD WOMAN

252. My hair was black, like the colour of bees, with curly ends; because of old age it is like bark fibres of hemp; not false is the utterance of the speaker of truth.

253. Covered with flowers my head was fragrant like a perfumed box; now because of old age it smells like a dog's fur; not false is the utterance of the speaker of truth.

254. Thick as a well-planted grove, made beautiful, having the ends parted by comb and pin; because of old age it is thin here and there; not false is the utterance of the speaker of truth.

255. Possessing fine pins, decorated with gold, adorned with plaits, it looked beautiful; because of old age that head has been made bald; not false is the utterance of the speaker of truth.

256. Formerly my eyebrows looked beautiful, like crescents well-painted by artists; because of old age they droop down with wrinkles; not false is the utterance of the speaker of truth.

257. My eyes were shining, very brilliant like jewels, very black and long; overwhelmed by old age they do not look beautiful; not false is the utterance of the speaker of truth.

258. In the bloom of my youth my nose looked beautiful like a delicate peak; because of old age it is like a flower-spike of long pepper; not false is the utterance of the speaker of truth.

259. My ear-lobes looked beautiful, like well-fashioned and well-finished bracelets; because of old age they droop down with wrinkles; not false is the utterance of the speaker of truth.

260. Formerly my teeth looked beautiful, like the colour of the bud of the plaintain; because of old age they are broken indeed and yellow; not false is the utterance of the speaker of truth.

261. Sweet was my warbling, like a cuckoo wandering in the grove in a jungle-thicket; because of old age it has faltered here and there; not false is the utterance of the speaker of truth..

262. Formerly my neck looked beautiful like a well-rubbed delicate conch-shell; because of old age it is broken and bowed-down; not false is the utterance of the speaker of truth.

263. Formerly both my arms looked beautiful, like round cross-bars; because of old age they are weak as the Pāṭalī tree; not false is the utterance of the speaker of truth.

264. Formerly my hands looked beautiful, with delicate signet rings, decorated with gold; because of old age they are like onions and radishes; not false is the utterance of the speaker of truth.

265. Formerly my breasts looked beautiful, swelling, round, close together, lofty; now they hang down like empty water-bags; not false is the utterance of the speaker of truth.

266. Formerly my body looked beautiful, like a well-polished sheet of gold; now it is covered with very fine wrinkles; not false is the utterance of the speaker truth.

267. Formerly both my thighs looked beautiful like an elephant's trunk; because of old age they are like stalks of bamboo; not false is the utterance of the speaker of truth.

268. Formerly my calves looked beautiful, possessing delicate anklets, decorated with gold; because of old age they are like sticks of sesame; not false is the utterance of the speaker of truth.

269. Formerly both my feet looked beautiful, like shoes full of cotton-wool; because of old age they are cracked, and wrinkled; not false is the utterance of the speaker of truth.

270. Such was this body; now it is decrepit, the abode of many pains; an old house, with its plaster fallen off; not false is the utterance of the speaker of truth.

Rohiṇī

271. "Lady, you fell asleep saying 'Ascetics'; you wake up saying 'Ascetics'; you praise only ascetics; assuredly you will be an ascetic.

272. You bestow much food and drink upon ascetics; Rohiṇī, now I ask you: Why are ascetics dear to you ?

273. Not dutiful, lazy, living on what is given by others; full of expectation, desirous of sweet things, why are ascetics dear to you ?"

274. "Truly for a long time you have been questioning me about ascetics, father; I shall praise to you their wisdom, virtuous conduct, and effort.

275. They are dutiful, not lazy, doers of the best of actions; they abandon desire and hatred; therfore ascetics are dear to me.

276. They shake off the three roots of evil, doing pure actions; all their evil is eliminated; therefore ascetics are dear to me.

277. Their body-activity is pure; and their speech-activity is likewise; their mind-activity is pure; therefore ascetics are dear to me.

278. They are spotless like mother-of-pearl, purified inside and out; full of good mental states; therefore ascetics are dear to me.

279. Having great learning, expert in the doctrine, noble, living in accordance with the doctrine; they teach the goal and the doctrine; therefore ascetics are dear to me.

280. Having great learning, expert in the doctrine, noble, living in accordance with the doctrine, with intent minds, they are possessed of mindfulness; therefore ascetics are dear to me.

281. Travelling far, possessed of mindfulness, speaking in moderation, not conceited, they comprehend the end of pain; therefore ascetics are dear to me.

282. If they go from any village, they do not look back longingly at anything; they go without longing indeed; therfore ascetics are dear to me.

283. They do not deposit their property in a store room, nor in a pot, nor in a basket, rather seeking that which is cooked; therfore ascetics are dear to me.

284. They do not take gold, coined or uncoined, or silver; they live by means of whatever turns up; therefore ascetics are dear to me.

285. Those who have gone forth are of various families and from various countries; nevertheless they are friendly to one another; therefore ascetics are dear to me.

286. "Truly for our sake, lady, you were born in our family, Rohiṇī; you have faith in the Buddha and the doctrine, and keen reverence for the Order.

287. You indeed comprehend this unsurpassed field of merit; these ascetics will receive our gift too. For among them an extensive sacrifice will be set up for us."

288. "If you are afraid of pain, if pain is unpleasant for you, go to the venerable Buddha as a refuge, to the doctrine, and to the Order; undertake the rules of virtuous conduct; that will be to your advantage."

289. "I go to the venerable Buddha as a refuge, to the doctrine, and to the Order; I undertake the rules of virtuous conduct; that will be to my advantage.

290. Formerly I was a kinsman of Brahmā, now I am truly a brahman. I possess the triple knowledge, and am versed in sacred lore, and have complete mastery of knowledge, and I am washed clean."

Cāpā

291. "Formerly I carried an ascetic's staff; now I am a deer-hunter;
because of craving I have not been able to go from the terrible
mire to that far shore.

292. Thinking me very enamoured of her, Cāpā has kept our son
happy; having cut Cāpā's bond I shall go forth again."

293. "Do not be angry with me, great hero; do not be angry with
me, great sage; for there is no purity for one overcome by
anger, how much less is there austerity."

294. "I shall indeed go out from Nālā; who will live here at Nālā ?
At Nālā women bind ascetics who live in accordance with the
doctrine, by means of their figure(s)."

295. "Come, Kāḷa, turn back, enjoy sensual pleasures as before; I
shall be under your control, and also whatever relatives I have." WOMAN

296. "If indeed a quarter of this were as you say, Cāpā, truly that AS SENSUAL
would be excellent for a man in love with you." ENTRAPMENT

297. "Kāḷa, like a sprouting Takkārī tree in flower on the crest of
a mountain, like a flowering Dālikā creeper, like a Pāṭalī tree in
the middle of an island,

298. with my body smeared with yellow sandalwood paste,
wearing my best muslin garments, being beautiful, why do you
go away abandoning me ?"

299. "Just as a fowler wishes to snare a bird, so do you by means
of your charming figure; but you will not fasten me."

300. "But this child-fruit of mine, Kāḷa, begotten by you, why do
you go away abandoning me with this child ?"

301. "Wise men leave their sons, and their relatives, and their
wealth; great heroes go forth, like an elephant which has
broken its fastening."

302. "Now I shall knock down to the ground on the spot this son THREAT
of yours, with stick or knife; because of grief for your son you TO
will not go." KILL SON

303. "If you give our son to the jackals and dogs, you will not turn me back again for the child's sake, you wretched one."

304. "Then fare you well now. Where will you go, Kāla? To what village, town, city, royal capital?"

305. "Formerly we were leaders of groups, not ascetics although thinking ourselves ascetics; we wandered from village to village, to cities and royal capitals.

306. But it will be different now, for the blessed one, the Buddha, alongside the River Nerañjarā, has taught the doctrine to living creatures for the abandonment of all pain. I shall go to his presence; he will be my teacher."

307. "You should utter my greeting now to the unsurpassed protector of the world; and having circumambulated him you should dedicate my gift."

308. "This is indeed proper for us, as you say, Cāpā; now I should utter your greeting to the unsurpassed protector of the world, and having circumambulated him I shall dedicate your gift."

309. And then Kāla went out alongside the River Nerañjarā; he saw the enlightened one teaching the state of the undying:—

310. pain, the uprising of pain, and the overcoming of pain, the noble eight-fold way leading to the stilling of pain.

311. He saluted his feet, circumambulated him, dedicated the gift for Cāpā, and went forth into the houseless state. He has obtained the three knowledges. He has done the Buddha's teaching.

Commentary says she renounces too

Sundarī

Father

312. "Lady, formerly when you caused to be eaten your sons who had passed away, you mourned excessively day and night.

313. Today, when you have caused seven children in all to be eaten, brahman-lady Vāseṭṭhī, why do you do not mourn greatly?"

Son dies-
Nun teaches father
Father renounces,
Then Sundarī

314. "Many hundreds of sons, and hundreds of groups of relatives of mine and yours have been caused to be eaten in the past, brahman.

315. Knowing the escape from birth and death, I do not grieve or lament; nor do I mourn."

ᚱ 316. "You speak such a truly amazing utterance, Vāseṭṭhī; whose doctrine do you know when you say such a thing ?"

√ 317. "That enlightened one, brahman, near the city of Mithilā, has taught the doctrine to living creatures for the abandonment of all pain.

318. I have heard that arahat's doctrine which is without basis for rebirth, brahman, and knowing the true doctrine there, I have thrust away grief for my son(s)."

319. "I too shall go near the city of Mithilā; perhaps that blessed one may release me from all pain."

320. The brahman saw the Buddha, completely released, without basis for rebirth. The sage who has reached the far shore of pain taught him the doctrine:—

321. pain, the uprising of pain, and the overcoming of pain, the noble eight-fold way leading to the stilling of pain.

322. Knowing the true doctrine there, he found pleasure in going forth; after three nights Sujāta attained the three knowledges.

ᚱ 323. "Come, charioteer, go, take back this chariot; bid the brahman-lady good health and say, 'The brahman has now gone forth. After three nights Sujāta has attained the three knowledges.'"

324. And then taking the chariot and 1,000 pieces too the charioteer bade the brahman-lady good health and said, "The brahman has now gone forth. After three nights Sujāta has attained the three knowledges."

325. "Hearing that the brahman has the triple knowledge, I give you this horse and chariot and 1,000 pieces too, a full bowl as a present for bringing good news."

326. "Keep the horse and chariot, and the 1,000 pieces too, brahman-lady; I too will go forth in the presence of the one who has excellent wisdom."

327. "Abandoning elephants, cows and horses, jewels and rings, and this rich domestic wealth, your father has gone forth. Enjoy enjoyments, Sundarī; you are the heir in the family."

328. "Abandoning elephants, cows and horses, jewels and rings, and this delightful domestic wealth, my father has gone forth, afflicted by grief for his son. I too shall go forth, afflicted by grief for my brother."

329. "May the intention, which you seek, prosper, Sundarī. Left-over scraps and gleanings as food, and a rag from a dust-heap as a robe, these are sufficient. You will be free from āsavas in the next world."

330. "Noble lady, the divine eye is purified as I undergo training; I know my former habitation, in which I lived before.

331. Relying on you, lovely one, beauty of the Order of therīs, I have obtained the three knowledges. I have done the Buddha's teaching.

332. Permit me, noble lady; I wish to go to Sāvatthi; I shall roar a lion's roar in the presence of the excellent Buddha."

333. "Sundarī, see the teacher, golden-coloured, with golden skin, the tamer of the untamed, the enlightened one, who has no fear from any quarter."

334. "See Sundarī coming, completely released, without basis for rebirth, rid of desire, unfettered, her task done, without āsavas."

335. "Gone out from Bārāṇasī, and come into your presence, your disciple Sundarī pays homage to your feet, great hero.

336. You are the Buddha, you are the teacher, I am your daughter, brahman, your true child, born from your mouth, my task done, without āsavas."

337. "Then welcome to you, good lady; you are not unwelcome. For in this way the tamed come, paying homage to the master's feet, rid of desire, unfettered, their task done, without āsavas."

Subhā, the smith's daughter

338. "I was young, with clean clothes, when previously I heard ʷᵉᵃˡᵗʰʸ the doctrine. Being vigilant, I obtained comprehension of the four truths.

339. Then I attained great non-delight in all sensual pleasures; seeing fear in individuality, I longed only for renunciation of the world.

340. I left the group of my relatives, the slaves, and servants, the rich fields and villages, and delightful and pleasant possessions, and I went forth, abandoning no small wealth.

341. Since I renounced the world in faith in this way, and the true doctrine has been well-preached, it would not be fitting for me, once I had laid aside gold and silver, to take them back again, for I desire the state of having nothing.

342. Silver or gold are not conducive to enlightenment or peace. This is not proper for ascetics; this is not the wealth of the noble ones.

343. This is being greedy, and intoxication, stupefaction, increase of defilement, full of suspicions and with many troubles; there is here no permanent stability.

344. Many men who are infatuated with this and careless, with defiled minds, being obstructed one by another, make a quarrel.

345. Slaughter, bonds, calamity, loss, grief and lamentation; much misfortune is seen for those who have fallen into sensual pleasures.

346. Why do you, my relatives, like enemies, urge on me towards sensual pleasures ? You know that I have gone forth, seeing fear in sensual pleasures.

347. The āsavas do not diminish because of gold, coined or uncoined; sensual pleasures are enemies, murderers, hostile, binding with ropes.

348. Why do you, my relatives, like enemies, urge on me towards sensual pleasures ? You know that I have gone forth, with shaven head, clad in the outer robe.

349. Left-over scraps and gleanings as food, and a rag from a dust-heap as a robe; this indeed is proper for me, the basic essentials for a houseless one.

350. The great seers have rejected sensual pleasures, those which are divine and those which are human. Those seers are completely released in the place of security; they have arrived at unshakable happiness.

351. May I not meet again with sensual pleasures, in which no refuge is found; sensual pleasures are enemies, murderers, like a mass of fire, painful.

352. Greed is an obstacle, full of fear, full of annoyance, full of thorns, and it is very disagreeable; it is a great cause of stupefaction.

353. Sensual pleasures are like a frightful attack, like a snake's head, which fools delight in, blind ordinary individuals.

354. For people are attached to the mud of sensual pleasures; many in the world are ignorant; they do not know the end of birth and death.

355. Because of sensual pleasures men enter very much upon the way which goes to a bad transition, bringing disease to themselves.

356. In this way sensual pleasures are enemy-producing, burning, defiling, the lures of the world, constraining, the bonds of death.

357. Sensual pleasures are maddening, deceiving, agitating the mind; a net spread out by Māra for the defilement of creatures.

358. Sensual pleasures have endless perils, they have much pain, they are great poisons, they give little enjoyment, they cause conflict, drying up the virtuous party.

359. Since I have caused such misfortune because of sensual pleasures, I shall not return to them again; I shall always delight in quenching.

360. Having been in conflict with sensual pleasures, being desirous of the cool state, I shall dwell vigilant, in the annihilation of their fetters.

361. I shall follow that griefless, stainless, secure, eight-fold, straight way, by which the great seers have crossed."

362. See this Subhā, the smith's daughter, standing firm in the doctrine. Having entered the immovable state she meditates at the foot of a tree.

363. Today is the eighth day. She went forth full of faith, beautiful by reason of the true doctrine, instructed by Uppalavaṇṇā, with triple knowledge, leaving death behind.

364. This one is a freed slave, without debt, a bhikkhunī with developed faculties, unfettered from all ties, her task done, without āsavas.

365. Sakka, the lord of beings, approaching by supernormal powers with a group of deities, reveres that Subhā, the smith's daughter.

THE GROUP OF THIRTY VERSES

Subhā Jīvakambavanikā

366. A rogue stopped the bhikkunī Subhā as she was going to the delightful Jīvakamba wood; Subhā said this to him:

367. "What wrong have I done you , that you should stand obstructing me ? For it is not fitting, sir, that a man should touch a woman who has gone forth.

368. This training was taught by the well-farer, in my teacher's severe teaching. Why do you stand obstructing me ? I possess the purified state, without blemish.

369. Why do you, with disturbed mind and with passion, stand obstructing me ? I am undisturbed, with passion departed, without blemish, with mind completely released in every respect."

370. "You arc young and not ugly; what will going-forth do for you ? Throw away your yellow robe. Come, let us delight in the flowery wood.

371. The towering trees send forth a sweet smell in all directions with the pollen of flowers; the beginning of spring is a happy season; come, let us delight in the flowery wood.

372. At the same time the trees with blossoming crests cry out, as it were, when shaken by the wind. What delight will there be for you if you plunge alone into the wood ?

373. You wish to go without companion to the lonely, frightening, great wood, frequented by herds of beasts of prey, disturbed by cow-elephants, who are excited by bull-elephants.

374. You will go about like a doll made of gold, like an acchara in Cittaratha. O incomparable one, you will shine with beautiful garments of fine muslin, with excellent clothes.

375. I should be at your beck and call if we were to dwell in the grove; for there is no creature dearer to me than you, o nymph with pleasant eyes.

376. If you will do my bidding, being made happy, come, live in a house; you will dwell in the calm of a palace; let women do attendance upon you.

377. Wear garments of fine muslin, put on garlands and unguents; I shall make much varied adornment for you, of gold, jewels, and pearls.

378. Climb on to a bed with a coverlet well-washed of dirt, beautiful, spread with a woollen quilt, new, very costly, decorated with sandalwood, having an excellent smell.

379. Just as a blue lotus with beautiful blossoms rising up from the water is touched by non-human water-spirits, so you, liver of the holy life, will go to old age with your limbs untouched by any man."

380. "What is it that you approve of as essential here in the body, which is full of corpses, filling the cemetery, destined to break up ? What is it that you have you seen when you look at me, being out of your mind ?"

381. "Your eyes are indeed like those of Turī, like those of a nymph inside a mountain; seeing your eyes my delight in sensual pleasures increases all the more.

382. Seeing your eyes in your face, to be compared with the bud of a blue lotus, spotless, like gold, my sensual pleasure increases all the more.

383. Even though you have gone far away, I shall remember you; you with the long eyelashes, you with the pure gaze; for no eyes are dearer to me than yours, you nymph with pleasant eyes."

384. "You wish to go by the wrong path; you seek the moon as a plaything; you wish to jump over Mt. Meru, you who have designs upon a child of the Buddha.

385. For I do not now have any object of desire anywhere in the world, including the deities; whatever sort it might be, it has been smitten root and all by the eight-fold way.

386. It has been scattered like sparks from a pit of burning coals; it is as valueless as a bowl of poison. Whatever sort it might be, it has been smitten root and all by the eight-fold way.

387. Try to seduce someone who has not observed this, or has not served the teacher; but if you seduce this one who knows, you will suffer distress.

388. For my mindfulness is established in the midst of both reviling and praise, happiness and pain; knowing that conditioned things are disgusting, my mind does not cling to anything at all.

389. I am a disciple of the well-farer, travelling in the eight-fold vehicle which is the way. With my dart drawn out, without āsavas, gone to a place of solitude, I rejoice.

390. For I have seen well-painted puppets, or dolls, fastened by strings and sticks, made to dance in various ways.

391. If these strings and sticks are removed, thrown away, mutilated, scattered, not to be found, broken into pieces, on what there would one fix the mind?

392. This little body, being of such a kind, does not exist without these phenomena; as it does not exist without phenomena, on what there would one fix one's mind?

393. Just as you have seen a picture painted on a wall, smeared with yellow orpiment; on that your gaze has been confused; so the wisdom of men is useless.

394. You blind one, you run after an empty thing, like an illusion ??? placed in front of you, like a golden tree at the end of a dream, like a puppet-show in the midst of the people.

395. An eye is like a little ball set in a hollow, having a bubble in the middle, with tears; there is eye secretion here too; various sorts of eyes are rolled into balls."

396. Removing her eye, the good-looking lady, with an unattached mind, was not attached to it. She said, "Come, take this eye for yourself." Straightway she gave it to this man.

397. And straightway his passion ceased there, and he begged her pardon. "Become whole again, liver of the good life. Such a thing will not happen again.

398. In smiting such a person, in embracing a blazing fire, I have seized a poisonous snake, as it were. Become whole again. Forgive me."

399. And then that bhikkhunī, released, went to the presence of the excellent Buddha. When she saw the one with the marks of excellent merit, her eye was restored to its former condition.

THE GROUP OF FORTY VERSES

Isidāsī

400. In the city named after a flower, Pāṭaliputta, in the best part of the earth, there were two bhikkhunīs, members of the Sakya clan, possessed of good qualities.

401. One of them was called Isidāsī; the second was called Bodhī. Both possessed virtue, delighted in meditation and study, and had great learning. They had shaken off defilements.

402. When they had wandered for alms, made their meal, and washed their bowls, seated happily in a lonely place, they uttered these words:

403. "You are lovely, noble Isidāsī, your youth has not yet faded. What fault have you seen in household life that you are then intent on renunciation of the world ?"

404. Asked in this way in the lonely place, Isidāsī, proficient in the teaching of the doctrine, said: "Hear, Bodhī, how I went forth.

405. In Ujjenī, best of cities, my father was a merchant, restrained by virtuous conduct. I was his only daughter, dear, and charming, and beloved.

406. Then from Sāketa came men, belonging to a most noble family, to woo me; a merchant with many jewels sent them. To him my father gave me as a daughter-in-law.

407. Approaching morning and evening I did obeisance with my head to my father-in-law and mother-in-law; I paid homage to their feet, as I had been instructed.

408. Seeing my husband's sisters, or his brothers, or his retinue, even my one and only beloved, I trembled and gave them a seat.

409. I gratified them with food and drink and hard food and whatever was stored there; I brought it forth and gave what was fitting to each.

410. Arising in good time I approached my lord's house; having washed my hands and feet, upon the threshold I approached my husband, with cupped hands.

411. Taking a comb, decorations, collyrium, and a mirror, I myself adorned my lord, like a servant-girl.

412. I myself prepared the rice-gruel; I myself washed the bowl; I looked after my husband as a mother her only son.

413. My husband offended against me, who in this way had show him devotion, an affectionate servant, with humbled pride, an early riser, not lazy, virtuous.

414. He said to his mother and father, 'I will take leave and go; I will not be able to live together with Isidāsī in one house.'   1st husb

415. 'Do not speak in this way, son; Isidāsī is learned, clever, an rejects her early riser, not lazy. Why does she not please you, son?'

416. 'She does me no harm, but I will not live with Isidāsī; to me she is just odious; I have had enough; having taken leave I will go.'

417. Hearing his utterance my father-in-law and mother-in-law asked me, 'What offence have you committed? Tell us confidently how it really was.'

418. 'I have not offended at all; I have not harmed him; I have not said any evil utterance; what can be done when my husband hates me?' I said.

419. Downcast, overcome by pain, they led me back to my father's house, saying, 'While keeping our son safe, we have lost the goddess of beauty incarnate.'

420. Then my father gave me to the kinsmen of a second rich man, belonging to a noble family, for half the bride-price for which the merchant had taken me. father marries her off again

421. In his house too I lived a month, then he too rejected me, although I served him like a slave-girl, not harming him, possessed of virtue.

422. And my father spoke to one who was wandering for alms, a tamer of others and self-tamed, 'Be my son-in-law; throw away your cloth and pot.'

423. He too, having lived with me for a fortnight, then said to my father, 'Give me my cloth and pot and cup; I will beg for alms again.'

424. Then my father, mother, and all the group of my relatives, 'What has not been done for you here ? Say quickly, what may be done for you.'

425. Spoken to in this way, he said, 'Even if I myself were honoured, I have had enough; I will not be able to live together with Isidāsī in one house.'

426. Allowed to go, he departed. I for my part, all alone, thought, 'I shall ask leave and go to die, or I shall go forth as a wanderer.'

427. Then the noble lady Jinadattā, expert in her discipline, with great learning, possessed of virtue, came to my father's house on her begging round.

428. Seeing her in our house, I rose up from my seat and offered it to her; I paid homage to her feet when she had sat down, and I gave her food.

429. I satisfied her completely with food and drink and hard food and whatever was stored there, and I said, 'Noble lady, I wish to go forth.'

430. Then my father said to me, 'Practise the doctrine in this very place, child; satisfy ascetics and twice-born brahmans with food and drink.'

431. Then lamenting and cupping my hands I said to my father, 'Evil indeed was the action I did; I shall destroy it.'

[handwritten margin note: SHE HAS AGENCY IN GOING FROM]

432. Then my father said to me, 'Attain enlightenment and the foremost doctrine, and obtain quenching, which the best of men realized.'

433. I saluted my mother and father, and all the group of my relatives, and seven days after going forth I attained the three knowledges.

434. I know my last seven births; I shall relate to you the (action) of which this is the fruit and result; listen to it with attentive mind.

[handwritten margin note: PAST LIVES]

435. In the city of Erakaccha I was a goldsmith, possessing much wealth. Intoxicated by pride in my youth, I had sexual intercourse with another's wife.

436. I fell from there, and was cooked in hell; I cooked for a long time; and rising up from there I entered the womb of a female monkey.

437. A great monkey, leader of the herd, castrated me when I was seven days old; this was the fruit of that action for me, because of having seduced another's wife.

438. I fell from there, and dying in the Sindhava forest, I entered the womb of a one-eyed, lame she-goat.

439. Castrated, and carrying children around for 12 years, I was worm-eaten, tail-less, unfit, because of having seduced another's wife.

440. I fell from there, and was born in a cow belonging to a cattle-dealer; a lac-red calf, castrated, for 12 months

441. I drew a great plough, and I pulled a cart, blind, tail-less, unfit, because of having seduced another's wife.

442. I fell from there, and was born of a household-slave in the street, as neither a woman nor a man, because of having seduced another's wife.

443. In my 30th year I died; I was born as a little girl in a carter's family, which was poor, with little wealth, much oppressed by creditors.

444. Then, because of the large amount of interest which had accumulated, a caravan-leader removed me from the family-house and dragged me off wailing.

445. Then in my 16th year, his son, Giridāsa by name, saw me as a maiden of marriageable age, and took me as his wife.

446. He had another wife, virtuous, possessed of good qualities, and famous, affectionate towards her husband; I stirred up enmity with her.

447. This was the fruit of that action for me, that they went rejecting me, although I served them like a slave-girl. Even of that I have now made an end.

THE GREAT GROUP OF VERSES

Sumedhā

448. In the city of Mantāvatī there was Sumedhā, a daughter of King Koñca's chief queen; she was converted by those who comply with the teaching.

449. Virtuous, a brilliant speaker, having great learning, trained in the Buddha's teaching, going up to her mother and father she said, "Listen, both of you. *[handwritten: she asks parents' permission]*

450. I delight in quenching; existence is non-eternal, even if it is as a deity; how much more non-eternal are empty sensual pleasures, giving little enjoyment and much distress.

451. Sensual pleasures, in which fools are bemused, are bitter, like a snake's poison. Consigned to hell for a long time, those fools are beaten, pained.

452. Because of evil action they grieve in a downward transition, being evil-minded, without faith; fools are unrestrained in body, speech, and mind.

453. Those fools, unwise, senseless, hindered by the uprising of pain, not knowing, do not understand the noble truths, when someone is teaching them.

454. They, the majority, not knowing the truths taught by the excellent Buddha, rejoice in existence [,mother]; they long for rebirth among the deities.

455. Even rebirth among the deities is non-eternal; it is in the impermanent existence; but fools are not afraid of being reborn again and again.

456. Four downward transitions and two upward transitions are obtained somehow or other; but for those who have gone to a downward transition there is no going-forth in the hells.

457. Permit me, both of you, to go forth in the teaching of the ten-powered ones; having little greed I shall strive for the elimination of birth and death.

458. What have I to do with existence, with delight, with this unsubstantial worst of bodies ? For the sake of the cessation of craving for existence, permit me, I shall go forth.

459. There is arising of Buddhas; the inopportune moment has been avoided; the opportune moment has been seized. As long as life lasts I would not infringe the rules of virtuous conduct and the living of the holy life."

460. So Sumedhā speaks to her mother and father; "Meanwhile I shall not take food as a householder; if I do not go forth I shall indeed have gone into the influence of death."

461. Pained, her mother laments; and her father, smitten by grief, strives to reconcile her, (as she lies) fallen to the ground on the roof of the palace.

462. "Stand up, child; what do you want with grieving ? You are bestowed. In Vāraṇavatī is King Anīkaratta, who is handsome; you are bestowed upon him.

463. You will be the chief queen, the wife of King Anīkaratta. The rules of virtuous conduct, the living of the holy life, going-forth, are difficult to perform, child.

464. In kingship there are orders to give, wealth, authority, happy enjoyments; you are young; enjoy the enjoyments of sensual pleasures; let your marriage take place, child."

465. The Sumedhā spoke to them, "May such things not be; existence is unsubstantial. Either there will be going-forth for me or death; not marriage.

466. Why should I cling to this foul body, impure, smelling of urine, a frightful water-bag of corpses, always flowing, full of impure things ?

467. What do I know it to be like? A body is repulsive, smeared with flesh and blood, food for worms, vultures, and other birds. Why is it given to us ?

468. The body is soon carried out to the cemetery, devoid of consciousness; it is thrown away like a log by disgusted relatives.

469. When they have thrown it away in the cemetery as food for others, one's own mother and father wash themselves, disgusted; how much more do common people ?

470. They are attached to the unsubstantial body, an aggregate of bones and sinews, to the foul body, full of saliva, tears, excrement, and urine.

471. If anyone, dissecting it, were to turn it inside out, even one's own mother, being unable to bear the smell of it, would be disgusted.

472. Reflecting in a reasoned manner that the elements of existence, the elements, the sense-bases are compounded, have rebirth as their root, and are painful, why should I wish for marriage ?

473. Let 300 newly sharpened swords fall on my body every day; even if the striking lasted 100 years it would be better, if in this way there were destruction of pain.

474. He should submit to this striking who in this way knows the teacher's utterance, 'Journeying-on is long for you, being killed again and again.'

475. Among deities and among men, in the womb of animals, and in the body of an asura, among ghosts and in hells, unlimited beatings are seen.

476. There are many beatings in hells for a defiled one who has gone to a downward transition. Even among the deities there is no protection; there is nothing superior to the happiness of quenching.

477. Those who are intent upon the teaching of the ten-powered one have attained quenching; having little greed they strive for the elimination of birth and death.

478. This very day, father, I shall renounce the world; what have I to do with unsubstantial enjoyments ? I am disgusted with sensual pleasures; they are like vomit, made groundless like a palm-tree."

479. In this way she spoke to her father, and at the same time Anīkaratta, to whom she was betrothed, surrounded by young men, came to the marriage at the appointed time.

480. The Sumedhā cut her black, thick, soft hair with a knife, closed the palace door, and entered on the first meditation.

481. Just as she entered on it, Anīkaratta arrived at the city; in that very palace Sumedhā developed notions of impermanence.

482. Just as she was pondering, Anīikaratta went up into the palace quickly. With his body adorned with jewels and gold, with cupped hands, he begged Sumedhā,

483. "In kingship there are (giving of) orders, wealth, authority, happy enjoyments; you are young; enjoy the enjoyments of sensual pleasures; happiness from sensual pleasures is hard to obtain in the world.

484. My kingship has been bestowed upon you; enjoy enjoyments; give gifts; do not be depressed; your mother and father are pained."

485. The Sumedhā, unconcerned with sensual pleasures, and free from delusion, said this: "Do not rejoice in sensual pleasures; see the peril in sensual pleasures.

486. Mandhātar, king of the four continents, was the foremost of those who had enjoyment of sensual pleasures. He died unsatified, not were his wishes fulfilled.

487. If the rainy one were to rain the seven jewels all around in the ten directions, there would still be no satisfaction with sensual pleasures; men die unsatisfied indeed.

488. Sensual pleasures are like a butcher's knife and chopping block; sensual pleasures are like a snake's head; they burn like a fire-brand; they are like a bony skeleton.

489. Sensual pleasures are impermanent, unstable; they have much pain, they are great poisons; they are like a heated ball of iron, the root of evil, having pain as the fruit.

490. Sensual pleasures are like the fruits of a tree, like lumps of flesh, painful; they are like dreams, delusive; sensual pleasures are like borrowed goods.

491. Sensual pleasures are like swords and stakes, a disease, a tumour, evil destruction, like a pit of coals, the root of evil, fear, slaughter.

492. In this way sensual pleasures have been said to have much pain, to be hindrances. Go ! I myself have no confidence in existence.

493. What will another do for me when his own head is burning ? When old age and death are following closely one must strive for their destruction."

494. Opening the door, and seeing her mother and father and Anīkaratta seated on the ground lamenting, she said this:

495. "Journey-on is long for fools and for those who lament again and again at that which is without beginning and end, at the death of a father, the slaughter of a brother, and their own slaughter.

496. Remember the tears, the milk, the blood, the journeying-on as being without beginning and end; remember the heap of bones of beings who are journeying-on.

497. Remember the four oceans compared with the tears, milk, and blood; remember the heap of bones of one man for one eon, equal in size to Mt. Vipula.

498. Remember the great earth, Jambudīpa, compared with that which is without beginning and end for one who is journeying-on. Split up into little balls the size of jujube kernels the number is not equal to his mother's mothers.

499. Remember the leaves, twigs, and grass compared with his fathers as being without beginning and end. Split up into pieces four inches long they are indeed not equal to his father's fathers.

500. Remember the blind turtle in the eastern sea, and the hole in the yoke to the west; remember the putting on of the yoke as a comparison with the obtaining of human birth.

501. Remember the form of this worst of bodies, unsubstantial, like a lump of foam. See the elements of existence as impermanent; remember the hells, giving much distress.

502. Remember those filling up the cemetery again and again in this birth and that. Remember the fears from the crocodile; remember the four truths.

503. When the undying exists, what do you want with drinking the five bitter things ? For all the delights in sensual pleasure are more bitter than the five bitter things.

504. When the undying exists, what do you want with sensual pleasures which are burning fevers ? For all delights in sensual pleasures are on fire, aglow, seething.

505. When there is non-enmity, what do you want with sensual pleasures which have much enmity ? Being similar to kings, fire, thieves, water, and unfriendly people, they have much enmity.

506. When release exists, what do you want with sensual pleasures, in which are slaughter and bonds ? For in sensual pleasures, unwilling, people suffer the pains of slaughter and

pleasures, unwilling, people suffer the pains of slaughter and bonds.

507. A grass fire-brand, when kindled, burns the one who holds it and does not let go; sensual pleasures are truly like fire-brands; they burn those who do not let go.

508. Do not abandon extensive happiness for the sake of a little happiness from sensual pleasures; do not suffer afterwards, like a puthuloma fish which has swallowed the hook.

509. Willingly, just control yourself among sensual pleasures. You are like a dog bound by a chain; assuredly sensual pleasures will treat you as hungry outcasts treat a dog.

510. Intent upon sensual pleasures you will suffer both unlimited pain and very many distresses of the mind; give up unstable sensual pleasures.

511. When the unageing exists, what do you want with sensual pleasures, in which are old age and death ? All births everywhere are bound up with death and sickness.

512. This is unageing, this is undying, this is the unageing, undying state; without grieving, without enmity, unobstructed, without stumbling, without fear, without burning.

513. This undying has been attained by many, and this is to be obtained even today by one who rightly applies himself; but it cannot be attained by one who does not strive."

514. So Sumedhā spoke, not obtaining delight in the constituent elements. Conciliating Anīkaratta, Sumedhā simply threw her hair on the ground.

515. Standing up Anīkaratta with cupped hands requested her father, "Let Sumedhā go, in order to go forth; she will be one with insight into the truths of complete release." [HUSBAND JOINS HER SIDE]

516. Allowed to go by her mother and father, she went forth, frightened by grief and fear; she realized the six supernormal powers while still undergoing training, and also the foremost fruit.

517. Marvellous, amazing was that quenching of the king's
daughter; as she explained at that last moment her activities in
her former habitations.

518. "In the time of the blessed one Koṇāgamana, in the Order's
pleasure park, in a new residence, we three friends, women,
gave a gift of a vihāra.

519. Ten times, one hundred times, ten hundred times, one
hundred hundred times we were reborn among the deities. But
what need is there to talk about rebirth among men ?

520. We had great supernormal powers among the deities. But
what need is there to talk about powers among mankind ? I was
the queen of a seven-jewelled king; I was his wife-jewel.

521. That was the cause, that the origin, that the root; that very
delight in the teaching, that first meeting, that was quenching
for one delighting in the doctrine."

522. So they say who have faith in the utterance of the one who
has perfect wisdom; they are disgusted with existence; being
disgusted with it they are disinterested in it.

INDEX OF NAMES

This index includes the names of persons and places which occur in the Therīgāthā and the commentary, and also the names of the therīs to whom verses are ascribed and to whom verses were uttered. When a therī's name occurs in her own verses (indicated by an asterisk prefixed to the verse number(s)) in the same form as in the rubric, the reference is not included. The numbers in bold type, given first, refer to verses. Those in lighter type refer to pages. The order is that of the Roman alphabet, and diacritical marks are disregarded.

Abhaya 23, 24
Abhayamātā *33-34
Abhayā *35-36, 24, 35
Abhirūpa-Nandā (= Nandā (1)) *19-20, 17, 44
Aciravatī (a river) 30
Aḍḍhakāsī *25-26, 19
Agni (a deity) 68
Āḷāra 2, 3
Āḷavī (a city) 33
Āḷavikā 154, 155
Āḷavikan 33
Ambapālī *252-70, 99
Ānanda 4, 25, 72
Ānanda (a king) 48
Anāthapiṇḍika 96, 154
Aṅga (a country) 110
Anīkaratta 462-63, 479, 481-82, 494, 514-15, 141, 144, 146, 151
Añjana 147, 69
Aññakoṇḍañña 3
Anomā (a river) 2
Anopamā *151-56, 70, 71
Antaka 188, 195, 203, 235
apaññātā bhikkhunī (1) (= Therikā) *1
apaññātā bhikkhunī (2) (= Sumaṅgalamātā) *23-24

apaññātā bhikkhunī (3) (= Vaḍḍhesī) *67-71
Aruṇa (a king) 24
Aruṇavā (a king) 35
Assaji 3
Avantī (a country) 135
Aviha (a hell) 110

Bandhumā (a king) 27
Bandhumatī (a city) 17, 27, 28, 104
Bārāṇasī (a city = Benares) 335
Benares (a city = Bārāṇasī) 3, 20, 37, 71, 72, 108, 111, 114, 115, 120, 128, 129
Bhaddaji 3
Bhaddavaggiyans 3
Bhaddā (1) Kāpilānī *63-66
Bhaddā (2) purāṇaniganthī *107-11 (= Kuṇḍalakesā)
Bhaddā 37, 38, 46, 51, 52, 53, 54, 55
Bhadrā *9
Bhaggava 2
Bhārukaccha (a city) 85
Bimbisāra (a king) 3, 23, 35, 66
Bodhi 401, 404, 134, 135
Bodhisatta 9
Brahmā (a deity) 290, 3
Brahma-god 2, 3

Brahma-heaven 38

Cālā *182-88, 79, 80, 81, 83,
158, 159
Candā *122-26, 61
Candabhāgā (a river) 8, 26, 29
Caṇḍāla 509
Cāpā *291-311, 108, 109, 110,
111, 112, 113, 114
Carabhūta 17
Channa 2
Cittā *27-28, 20
Cittaratha 374
Culla 20

Dantikā *48-50, 29
Devadaha 40, 72
Dhammā *17, 15
Dhammadinnā *12, 7, 12, 13, 32,
40
Dhammapāla 153
Dhīrā (1) *6, 13, 16
Dhīrā (2) *7, 10
Dīpaṅkara (a buddha) 1

Erakaccha 435

Ganges (a river) 93, 134
Gayā 3
Ghaṭīkāra (a Brahma-god) 2
Gijjhakūṭa 108
Giridāsa 445, 134, 140
Gotama (a buddha) 136, 155,
162, 71
Gotama (family name) 72
Gotamid 7, 9, 21, 22, 29, 38, 40,
71, 72, 121, 126, 156
Gotamī (gotta) see Mahāpajāpati
*157-62
Gotamī (family name) 88, 89, 156
Guttā *163-68, 74

Haṃsavatī (a city) 12, 30, 33, 37,
44, 48, 50, 51, 55, 66, 71, 88, 92

Inda (a deity) 121
India 148
Isidāsī *400-47, 134, 135, 136,
137, 138
Isipatana 3, 72

Jain 51
Jambudīpa 498
Jentā 18
Jentī *21-22, 18
Jetavana 29, 38, 48, 53, 57, 67,
72, 90, 92, 109, 154
Jinadattā 427, 134
Jīva 51; -sanāmikā 51
Jīvā 30, 31
Jīvaka 126, 127
Jīvakambavana 366
Jīvakambavanikā see Subhā (2)
*366-99

Kakusandha 32, 66, 96
Kāla 2
Kāḷa 295, 297, 300, 304, 309
Kāḷudāyi 3
Kāmaloka 83
kammāradhītā see Subhā (1) *338-
65
Kammāsadamma (a city) 46, 47
Kanthaka 2
Kapila(n) 37, 38
Kāpilānī see Bhaddā (1) *63-66
Kapilavatthu (a city) 3, 9, 17, 22,
44
Kāsī (a city) 110, 12, 20, 52;
-janapada 25
Kāsika 374, 377
Kassapa (a buddha) 6, 12, 19, 37,
48, 51, 55, 66, 71, 96, 141
Kassapa (an elder) 63, 38
Khemā *139-44, 66, 67, 75
Khemaka 17
Kiki (a king) 12, 52, 55, 66
Kisā-Gotamī *213-23

Konāgamana (a buddha) 6, 32, 66, 96, 141, 151
Koñca (a king) 141
Kosala (a country) 110, 11, 14, 28, 30
Kosambī (a city) 25, 26
Kosiya 38
Kurus (a people) 46, 47
Kuṇḍalakesā (= Bhaddā (2)) 518,

Lacchī 419
Licchavis (a people) 18
Lumbinī 1

Magadha (a country) 110, 2, 23, 66, 79
Mahā-Moggallāna 41, 46
Mahānāma 3
Mahāpajāpatī Gotamī *157-62, 44
Mahā-Suppabuddha 72
Mahātittha (a village) 38
Majjha 151, 70
Mandhātar (a king) 486, 147
Mantāvatī (a city) 448, 141
Māra 7, 10, 56, 65, 164, 231, 357, 2, 10, 11, 34, 35, 67, 79, 80, 81, 83, 84, 85, 94, 154, 155, 156, 157, 158, 159, 160, 161, 162, 163
Māyā 162, 72, 73
Meru 384, 130
Mettā (= Mittā (2)) *31-32
Mettikā *29-30, 21
Mithilā (a city) 135, 317, 319, 64, 65, 114, 116, 117
Mittā (1) *8
Mittā (2) *31-32
Mittakālī *92-96, 47
Moggallāna 3
Muttā (1) *2, 7
Muttā (2) *11, 11

Nāga 2
Nālā 294

Nālaka 79
Nanda 4, 17, 44
Nandā (1) (= Abhirūpa-Nandā) *19-20, 17, 18
Nandā (2) (= Sundarī-Nandā) *82-86, 44
Nandā 48
Nandaka 4, 72
Nandamūlaka 71
Nanduttarā *87-91, 46
Nerañjarā (a river) 306, 309, 113
Niganthas 46, 53
Nimmānaratino (deities) 197-98

Oghāṭaka 11

Padara-Tittha-Vihāra 153
Padumavatī 23
Padumuttara (a buddha) 12, 30, 37, 44, 48, 50, 51, 55, 66, 71, 88, 92
Pajāpatī 4, 6, 7, 8, 9, 17, 21, 22, 29, 38, 40, 44, 72, 73, 74, 121, 126
Pakulā 48
Pañcasatā Paṭācārā *127-32
Paṇḍava 2
Pasenadi (a king) 15
Paṭācārā *112-16, [117-21], 119, 125, [127-32], 178, 27, 57, 58, 59, 60, 61, 63, 77, 78
Pāṭaliputta (a city = Patna) 400
Patna (a city = Pāṭaliputta) 134, 135
Phussa 12
Pippali 38
Puṇṇā (1) *3, 8
Puṇṇā (2) (= Puṇṇikā) *236-51
Puṇṇikā (= Puṇṇā (2)) *236-51

Rāhu- 2
Rāhula 4, 44
Rājagaha (a city) 54, 226, 2, 4, 12, 13, 21, 24, 29, 32, 35, 52, 75, 93, 121, 126

Vaḍḍhamātā *203-12
Vaḍḍhesī (= apaññātā bhikkhunī
(3)) *67-71, 40
Vagga 20
Vajirā 162, 163
Vajjī 110
Vaṅkahāra 108, 109
Vappa 3
Vāraṇavatī (a city) 462, 142
Vasavattino (deities) 197-98
Vāseṭṭhī (= Vāsiṭṭhī) *133-38,
313, 316, 115, 117
Vesālī 4, 6, 18, 41, 42, 64, 72, 99,
104, 105
Vessabhu (a buddha) 32, 96, 114
Vijayā *169-74, 75, 157
Vimala-Koṇḍañña 99
Vimalā purāṇagaṇikā *72-76, 41
Vipassi (a buddha) 17, 22, 26, 27,
28, 32, 66, 96, 104
Vipula 497, 148
Visākha 7, 12
Visākhā *13

Yakkha 23
Yāmā (deities) 197-98, 141
Yasa 3